MEXICO UNDER ZEDILLO

A Publication of the Americas ✖ *Society*

MEXICO UNDER ZEDILLO

WITHDRAWN

EDITED BY
SUSAN KAUFMAN PURCELL
& LUIS RUBIO

LYNNE
RIENNER
PUBLISHERS

BOULDER
LONDON

Published in the United States of America in 1998 by
Lynne Rienner Publishers, Inc.
1800 30th Street, Boulder, Colorado 80301

and in the United Kingdom by
Lynne Rienner Publishers, Inc.
3 Henrietta Street, Covent Garden, London WC2E 8LU

Library of Congress Cataloging-in-Publication Data
Mexico under Zedillo /   edited by Susan Kaufman Purcell and Luis Rubio.
    p. cm.
    Includes bibliographical references and index.
    Contents: Coping with political change—Luis Rubio / Crisis and
economic change in Mexico—Mauricio A. González Gómez / Political
dilemmas of welfare reform—Guillermo Trejo and Claudio Jones /
The new U.S.-Mexico relationship—Susan Kaufman Purcell.
    ISBN 1-55587-315-4 (alk. paper)
    1. Mexico—Politics and government—1988– 2. Mexico—Economic
conditions. 3. Mexico—Social conditions. 4. Zedillo Ponce de
León, Ernesto. I. Purcell, Susan Kaufman. II. Rubio-Freidberg,
Luis.
F1236.M496 1998
972.08'35—dc21   97-32753
                                                                         CIP

British Cataloguing in Publication Data
A Cataloguing in Publication record for this book
is available from the British Library.

Printed and bound in the United States of America

The paper used in this publication meets the requirements
of the American National Standard for Permanence of
Paper for Printed Library Materials Z39.48-1984.

5 4 3 2 1

Contents

Illustrations

Figures

Tables

Foreword

Mexico today is a very different country from the Mexico of only a decade ago. In this relatively brief period, its leaders have transformed the country's formerly state-dominated economy into one that is now highly integrated into the new global economy. Tariffs and other barriers to imports have fallen drastically or disappeared. The process of privatization has transferred important companies from the public to the private sector, and the once inward-oriented economy has been transformed into one in which exports are of great and still growing importance.

These changes did not come easily. They began as a response to the 1982 debt crisis and Mexico's consequent inability to continue pursuing its costly statist development strategy. The economic transformation was initiated at the top, by the leadership of Mexico's essentially authoritarian political regime, and initially lacked broad popular support. Mexico's entry into the North American Free Trade Agreement (NAFTA) in late 1993 both symbolized the country's commitment to a new kind of economy and helped ensure the sustainability of the economic reforms. Although not everyone in Mexico is pleased by the country's new economic direction, which involves ever greater interdependence with the United States, even opposition political leaders now acknowledge that there is no going back to Mexico's economic past.

The economic reforms also accelerated the pace of Mexico's political opening. By reducing the role of the state in the economy, the governing party was deprived of important resources and patronage that had traditionally been essential in guaranteeing its continued rule. The midterm elections of July 1997, which cost the Institutional Revolutionary Party (PRI) its control of Congress while electing an opposition party leader mayor of Mexico City, proved that political power in Mexico had indeed become more diffused and the country more pluralistic and democratic.

Mexico's recent history, however, is not one of unmitigated triumphs. Along the way, the gap between the rich and poor increased; economic stabilization programs made life very difficult even for the middle classes; political violence took the life of the PRI's intended candidate in the 1994 elections, as well as other party officials; and evidence of growing penetration of drug interests into the political fabric continued to accumulate. Finally, the economic and political changes in Mexico, which had produced an important convergence of interests between Mexico and the United States in many areas, also made bilateral relations between the two countries more complicated and difficult to manage.

Mexico Under Zedillo examines all these developments and their implications for both Mexico's future and the future of U.S.-Mexico relations. It is a timely book about a country whose importance to the United States and its citizens continues to grow. Its insights into the relationship between economic and political liberalization and the implementation of free trade agreements also make it relevant to a fuller understanding of both the opportunities and constraints involved in the creation of a Free Trade Area of the Americas by the year 2005, a goal that is shared by both the United States and its hemispheric neighbors.

Everett Ellis Briggs
President, Americas Society

Acknowledgments

This book reflects the combined efforts of a number of individuals and organizations. We especially want to thank the members of the 1994 study group, "Mexico After the NAFTA," who contributed their knowledge and insights regarding Mexico's economic and political reforms and their impact on social policy and U.S.-Mexican relations. We also profited from a discussion group organized by the Centro de Investigación para el Desarrollo, A.C. (CIDAC), in Mexico City in 1996.

We particularly want to thank Ambassador Jorge Pinto, Mexico's consul general in New York, for his helpful comments on an earlier draft of the chapters included in the book. We also greatly appreciate the help of Stephanie Crane, Ross Culverwell, and Heather Ward, former assistants to the vice president of the Americas Society, for their help in organizing and running the study group. The assistance of Alex Gross, the current associate program officer in the Office of the Vice President, and Abigail Paige, current assistant to the vice president, has been invaluable in the preparation of the manuscript for publication. In addition, we wish to thank Michelle Miller-Adams for her excellent editorial work. Finally, we would like to acknowledge the staff at Lynne Rienner Publishers for their important contributions to the editorial and publication processes.

This book and the study group from which it developed were made possible by generous grants to the Department of Latin American Affairs of the Americas Society by the Tinker Foundation and the William and Flora Hewlett Foundation.

Susan Kaufman Purcell
Luis Rubio

Acronyms and Abbreviations

CGPE	General Economic Policy Criteria
CIDAC	Research Center for Development
CIDE	Center for Research and Teaching in Economics
CNM	National Coordinator of Teachers
CTM	Confederation of Mexican Workers
DEA	Drug Enforcement Agency
DRLD	Categories of insurance services under the original social security fund (i.e., disabilities, retirement, laid-off senior employees, and death)
EPR	Popular Revolutionary Army
ESF	Exchange Stabilization Fund
EZLN	Zapatista Army of National Liberation
FDN	National Democratic Front
FGT Index	Foster Greer Thorbecke Index
FONHAPO	National Fund for Popular Housing
FOVISSSTE	Housing Fund for State Workers
FSTSE	Federation of State Workers
FTAA	Free Trade Area of the Americas
GATT	General Agreement on Tariffs and Trade
GDP	gross domestic product
GEA	Group of Economists and Associates
GNP	gross national product
IMF	International Monetary Fund
IMSS	Mexican Social Security Institute
INEGI	National Institute of Geographic and Informational Statistics
INFONAVIT	Institute of the Workers Housing Fund
INI	National Indigenous Institute
INS	Immigration and Naturalization Service

ISI	import-substitution industrialization
ISSSTE	State Workers Social Security Institute
NAFTA	North American Free Trade Agreement
OECD	Organization for Economic Cooperation and Development
PAN	National Action Party
PND	National Development Plan
PNR	National Revolutionary Party
PRD	Party of the Democratic Revolution
PRI	Institutional Revolutionary Party
PRM	Party of the Mexican Revolution (now the PRI)
PROCAMPO	Agricultural Production Benefits Program
PROGRESA	Food, Health, and Education Program
PRONASOL	National Solidarity Program
SAR	Retirement Savings System
SEDESOL	Ministry of Social Development
SEM	single European market
SEP	Ministry of Education
SNTE	National Union of Educational Workers
SPP	Ministry of Budget and Planning
SS	Ministry of Health
UDI	indexed investment units

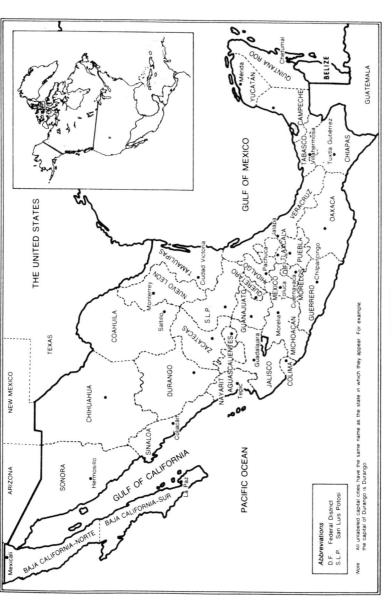

MEXICO

Reprinted from *Politics in Developing Countries: Comparing Experiences with Democracy*, 2d ed., edited by Larry Diamond, Juan J. Linz, and Seymour Martin Lipset. Copyright © 1995 by Lynne Rienner Publishers and the National Endowment for Democracy.

Introduction

Susan Kaufman Purcell and Luis Rubio

Ernesto Zedillo Ponce de León became Mexico's president on December 1, 1994, following a year of extraordinary political turmoil in Mexico. The year began with the sudden appearance of an armed guerrilla group in Chiapas, the country's most southern state. In March the governing party's presidential candidate was murdered, and only six months later, another high-ranking party official was assassinated. Although the July presidential elections were peaceful and the most honest in Mexico's history, within three weeks of President Zedillo's inauguration the peso collapsed. The new Mexican president therefore began his six-year term confronting an extremely serious economic crisis that threatened the stability of the country's political system as well.

Despite many dire predictions, however, the economic reforms begun in the 1980s remain largely intact, and economic growth has resumed. Perhaps even more surprising, the political system today is considerably more democratic in the aftermath of the July 1997 midterm elections, which deprived the governing party of its traditional control of Congress and put an opposition party leader in control of Mexico City. Attention is now focused on the presidential election of 2000, which could produce another first—the election of an opposition party candidate as president of Mexico.

This book examines the many ways in which Mexico has changed during the Zedillo presidency, placing the most recent reforms in the context of the earlier efforts of the president's most immediate predecessors. It results from a series of papers first commissioned for a study group that met at the Americas Society in New York during 1994. The December 1994 peso devaluation and the ensuing uncertainty and unrest made it necessary for the authors to totally rewrite their chapters, which they did in 1996–1997. The

1

study group participants included individuals from business, government, journalism, and academia, both from Mexico and the United States. Although the first drafts of the chapters were discussed during the meetings of the study group, as a result of the extensive rewriting, the published book reflects the personal views of the individual authors and not those of the study group itself.

In the first chapter, "Coping with Political Change," Luis Rubio looks at Mexico's transition from an authoritarian regime characterized by an extremely strong presidency to a more pluralistic democratic system in which political power is more evenly distributed between the president and Congress and among the federal, state, and local levels of government. Rubio argues that to date, the components of the authoritarian system have been weakened, and strong, new democratic institutions have not yet developed to take their place. He gives particular importance to the need to establish the rule of law in order to consolidate Mexican democracy but concludes that his country has made progress in moving in that direction under President Zedillo's leadership.

In Chapter 2, Mauricio A. González Gómez discusses the economic reform process that began in Mexico in the aftermath of the 1982 debt crisis. He focuses on the macroeconomic changes and structural reforms that have been implemented as well as the social policies that have been put in place by President Zedillo and his two immediate predecessors. Whether Mexico will be able to sustain growth in both export-oriented and domestic market–oriented sectors remains an open question for him. In order to achieve these goals, he argues for additional reforms in the financial and agricultural sectors as well as new education and industrial policies.

Chapter 3, by Guillermo Trejo and Claudio Jones, examines Mexico's social welfare policies in the context of the economic and political changes that the country has experienced since the early 1980s. The authors are disturbed by the growing inequality of income as well as the increasing disparity between levels of development in the country's north and south that have accompanied Mexico's economic reform process. They also question whether increased democracy will be able to correct this situation. Their chapter includes specific discussions of education, health, housing, poverty alleviation, and safety-net policies that have been implemented in recent years. In their conclusion they emphasize the need for more citizen participation through democratic institutions in order to produce greater well-being for the majority of Mexicans.

In the final chapter, Susan Kaufman Purcell examines the ways in which Mexico's entry into the North American Free Trade Agreement (NAFTA) and the country's transition to democracy have changed bilateral relations between the United States and Mexico. Specifically, she argues that NAFTA has greatly blurred the line between domestic and foreign policymaking in both countries. At the same time, greater democracy in Mexico means that the country's policy toward the United States will increasingly reflect the diversity of views and interests within Mexico. As a result of both developments, bilateral relations between the United States and Mexico have become more complicated and difficult to manage, a trend that will continue. At the same time, the growing convergence of interests in certain areas between the two countries will help offset some of the new challenges.

1

Coping with Political Change

Luis Rubio

Mexican society is in flux—each of its traditional parameters has been altered over the past several decades. There has been a qualitative transformation in the nature of demands on the government as well as an extraordinary explosion in the strength of the media. Fundamental institutions of state and society have collapsed, as is evident in growing problems of personal security. Perhaps even more striking than the degree of change is that there is no end in sight to the turmoil that has characterized Mexican politics in recent years. The changes under way may take Mexico in any number of directions. And although most Mexicans welcome change in the abstract (which they identify with higher incomes, better standards of living, and less abuse by the various layers of bureaucrats they have to deal with), they are concerned about the continuing uncertainty that plagues their political and economic system.

In this chapter I analyze the political dilemmas currently facing Mexico. The first section describes the overall contours of national politics, sketching the developments that led to Mexico's current situation and posing the main questions that affect the political process. In the second section I examine the political system more closely, focusing on the structure and functions of Mexico's traditional political institutions and analyzing how they began to unravel. This section also considers the evolution of the Mexican presidency to determine whether the current president's actions or inactions lie at the core of today's problems, or whether he has in fact adopted a strategy that will succeed in transforming the country. The third section addresses the crucial question of how Mexico's political parties will cope with ongoing change and illustrates a central dilemma: although Mexico's parties were able to agree on new rules for electoral competition that signaled a dramatic departure from the old political system and the governing Institutional Revolutionary Party (PRI) adopted stringent internal regulations that directly challenge the assumptions behind those agreements, there is no consensus among the country's politicians or parties on anything beyond the electoral realm. In the absence of key institutions to deal with political conflict, Mexico could find itself with the hardware of democracy (i.e., elections, a judiciary) but without the software of governance to make it work (i.e., rule of law, an independent media, a professional bureaucracy, etc.). To consider how this situation can be avoided, in the final section I turn my attention to the future, describing the new factors that play a role in the political scene, such as international and transborder political coalitions and the explosion in the availability of information, domestic as well as foreign. I also analyze potential scenarios for Mexico's electoral future and assess the potential for ongoing disruption of the political process.

The main argument of the chapter is that Mexico has been experiencing profound change since the 1960s at all levels: in society, in the economy, and in political life. These changes result from both the normal evolution of society (demographics, increased levels of education, changes in the urban-rural balance, and increased availability of information) and government policy, particularly in the economy. These changes altered the traditional balance of a very steady political system but have failed to set Mexico on the path of sustainable economic growth. Economic reforms have been bold and ambitious, but they have been insufficient to attain their avowed objectives. More important, those reforms undermined or destroyed the old institutions that preserved stability (and the PRI monopoly of power). Thus, the old institutions have not been replaced by new ones capable of coping with the new political forces that the reforms themselves have unleashed. I end the chapter with the proposition that, in the absence of a consensus on the future, the country needs strong institutions to ensure that there is a process to which all political actors subscribe, such as the rule of law. Only with such common ground will Mexico remain a stable nation, capable of advancing toward new stages of political and democratic development.

Roots of the Current Turmoil

The majority of Mexicans living today have never known a period of stability. The student movement of 1968 inaugurated an era of convulsions that has not yet come to an end. Prior to 1968, Mexicans enjoyed what was known as the "Mexican miracle," under which the country experienced social and political peace along with exceptionally high rates of economic growth (averaging over 7 percent from 1952 to 1970, and in several of those years exceeding 10 percent). The 1968 student movement constituted a watershed not because of the students' aims or even the violence with which it ended, but because it revealed that Mexico's social and political peace was less the result of consensus and social satisfaction than it was the product of a set of authoritarian practices and institutions that were starting to break down. Beginning with the administration of Luis Echeverría Álvarez (1970–1976), one Mexican government after another has sought to come to terms with the political problems that erupted in 1968, as well as the economic consequences of the policies that emerged in response to them.

Mexico's current turmoil has three broad sources: an unfinished economic reform agenda and its social consequences; a political system, built in the 1920s for the conditions of that era, that has failed to come to terms with a new reality; and the clashes of ideologies, interests, and objectives among a growing number of social actors with ever wider agendas. These factors share a common denominator. Mexico has for many years been in the process of abandoning its traditional structures, institutions, and safety nets, but these have not yet been replaced by a stable alternative. The concept of transition implies an eventual point of arrival; perhaps the biggest problem for Mexico today is the striking lack of consensus over the ultimate objectives of the current transition.

For the past twenty-five years, one Mexican government after another has tried to address the problems outlined in the previous paragraph. Some of these efforts have made the problems worse or created new ones. The economy, which had thrived in the 1950s and 1960s, deteriorated in the 1970s. Misguided government policies hindered the country's ability to adjust early on to changes in the international economy while increasing the external debt. The approach of the Echeverría and López Portillo (1976–1982) administrations was to increase levels of public spending, financing this activity through foreign loans and inflation. Not only did this strategy fail to address the political problems that had surfaced in 1968, but it produced economic chaos from which the economy has not yet recovered.

Miguel de la Madrid Hurtado (1982–1988) and later Carlos Salinas de Gortari (1988–1994) introduced far-reaching economic reforms that, in retrospect, signified the beginning of a shift from a government-centered system to one with a higher degree of societal involvement. But their policies, generally sound in the economic arena, failed to accommodate an increasingly active society that lacked the institutional mechanisms to channel its grievances and demands. The inflationary policies and economic isolationism of the 1970s coupled with the profound economic reforms from 1980 to 1995 removed most of the protections enjoyed by Mexican industry. This further undermined Mexico's traditional political institutions without creating new ones.

De la Madrid and Salinas sought to transform the economic foundations of the country and make the Mexican economy competitive internationally. Privatization of state-owned companies, deregulation, and import liberalization served as levers to increase efficiency and raise productivity; officials also hoped that these measures would raise the income of the average Mexican. Although these policies have gone a long way toward creating a new economic structure, one in which exports have increased to unprecedented levels, their success is confined only to part of Mexico's economy and society. The winners in this process have been those companies (and regions) that have modernized, upgraded their plant and equipment, and retrained their personnel; they now see the world as their market. The losers come from the old industry, typically based on import-substitution industrialization, which became fashionable after World War II and was heavily dependent on government subsidies and protection from imports. The winners are mostly located in the north and west of the country, but there are many such firms throughout the nation; they represent about 60 percent to 70 percent of industrial production, even though they number no more than 15,000 firms and employ about 30 percent to 40 percent of industrial labor. The overwhelming majority of firms are among the losers, are typically located not too far from Mexico City, and employ about 60 percent of industrial labor. All of these firms have shown themselves unable—and often unwilling—to adjust or compete.

The economy represents only one aspect of Mexico's current dilemma. When the political system was organized in the 1920s, the PRI could legitimately claim to represent most Mexicans. This is no longer true today, as can be assessed by the growth of the National Action Party (PAN) and the Party of the Democratic Revolution (PRD) through the 1990s and, in particular, by the midterm federal elections of 1997. Thus, the traditional political system is no longer representative, nor is it effective either in channeling demands or making decisions. The government has lost credibility, and Mexicans—from the Zapatista rebels to labor unions, from the PRI to the church—have found new ways to challenge its authority. Even the most loyal members of the old guard have sought to distance themselves from the government. This disaffection reflects the fact that, although Mexico has invested considerable effort in restructuring the economy, little attention has been given to addressing the political side of the equation. The hope has been that a successful economic revival will help the government weather the political storm or at least manage it from a position of strength.

The political problems that have long plagued the country are now taking center stage. Whatever the rationale for avoiding them in the past, the fact remains that they have become ever bigger and more complex over time. The old political system has proven incapable of anticipating events or of developing a set of institutions capable of absorbing the negative consequences of economic reform. As farsighted as some of Mexico's recent presidents may have been, particularly in the economic sphere, each reacted to events rather than anticipating them; each responded inadequately to the challenges that arose; and each had one fundamental goal—to be deemed a success during his own term in office.

The only realm where consistent and far-reaching reform has been taking place is the economy. Even though it has as yet failed to secure benefits for most Mexicans, it is the only area where there has been consistency. In fact, the reforms undertaken since 1982 and still being pursued today were designed to transform the Mexican economy and provide a foundation for long-term growth and development. These goals may well be met, although not evenly distributed in the immediate future. In retrospect, by failing to address the political component of Mexico's problems, the reformers tied their own hands. They took advantage of the Mexican presidency's extraordinary powers to launch very ambitious and politically sensitive reforms. By the same token, they found it unnecessary to build a constituency to sustain the reforms. This thrust had the advantage of being expedient but the disadvantage of not addressing key constituencies, many of which ended up rebelling against the reforms at the first opportunity they had. Furthermore, by disregarding the opposition, reformers made many mistakes that might have been avoided. Checks and balances are costly and complex, but they have proven to be crucial to the permanence of reforms. In this sense, without the political consensus necessary to pursue their economic objectives, these have been only partially successful. At the same time, the reformers' inaction on the political front also strengthened the opposition, raising questions about the viability of political reform.

Several points are clear: what has happened in Mexico both in

the economy and in politics since reform began in the 1980s is not
what the government expected, anticipated, or desired. The government aimed to produce a strong and sustained economic recovery
while leaving the political system untouched (and, if possible,
strengthened). What it got instead was a split economy, high levels
of unemployment, and a shaky political system. In this context, the
North American Free Trade Agreement (NAFTA) has become critical, for it is the strongest political institution at hand to guide the
economy. While it is crucial for sustaining the reforms already in
place, NAFTA is not enough to provide the long-term certainty that
change will occur within a predictable framework. Only the establishment of the rule of law could ensure stability throughout
Mexico's reform process.

Perhaps more important, recent reformers' lack of success in
fundamentally altering the contours of Mexican politics and economics suggests that they assumed they were dealing with a controlled economy, while, in fact, they were faced with circumstances
beyond their control, both within Mexico and in the world at large.
The problem appears to be not just one of finding the appropriate
policies; rather, Mexico lacks the institutions necessary to accommodate itself to a changing world. The task of constructing these institutions is the primary one facing Mexico's current and future political leadership.

The Political System, Old and New

Two principles have guided Mexico's postrevolutionary political
system. One was the exchange of loyalties for political and economic
gain. The other was the supremacy of the presidency. These traits
not only characterized Mexico for decades but also go a long way
toward explaining both the longevity of the PRI and of the political
arrangements that lie at its core. They are also helpful in understanding the country's economic ascent from the 1940s to the early
1970s, as well as its current troubles.

The core institution of the political system after the 1920s was
the presidency. Regardless of the formal structure of the system, the
presidency was its centerpiece. Almost every institution and entity
was built to interact with it, serving either as a mechanism through
which societal groups negotiated with the president or as an instrument for presidential action. Though a host of formal governmental
structures existed, from the legislature to political parties, all operated around the presidency. The presidency gained its central position
immediately after the revolutionary years, when a series of *hombres*

fuertes (strongmen) and *caciques* (political bosses) emerged, leading to a concentration of political and military power. Álvaro Obregón (1920–1924) was the first of the strongmen, but it was Plutarco Elías Calles (1924–1928) who shaped the political system by creating the National Revolutionary Party (PNR), which became the Party of the Mexican Revolution (PRM) and eventually was transformed into the PRI.

Calles constructed an exceptional piece of political engineering. He succeeded not only in drawing into a single organization virtually all of Mexico's then-relevant political groups—parties, militias, unions, and politicians—but also in creating a mechanism whereby all of them benefited from continued participation. As the party evolved, its foremost traits became clear. The first of these was the central role played by successive presidents. From 1928 to 1934 the presidency was held by three of Calles's subordinates—Emilio Portes Gil, Pascual Ortiz Rubio, and Abelardo Rodríguez. Calles was ousted as national political boss by his successor, Lázaro Cárdenas (1934–1940). With that, power was transferred to the incumbent, who, in turn, used it to force all politics into the newly created party. The president was barred from being reelected and thus became what one observer has called a "non-hereditary monarchy." The party became institutionalized, giving way to a continuous shift in coalitions. One president after another served as the centerpiece of the system, each sustained in power by a different coalition. The president was undisputed leader during his term, but this privilege lasted only for that period. The periodic change in coalitions served as a kind of "oxygen" for the system as a whole, ensuring that it remained representative and legitimate in the eyes of most societal groups. At the end of the day, the key to control of the system rested on the president's extraordinary influence on the nomination of his successor. That power allowed him to reward or punish any politician or group throughout his term and was the single most effective control mechanism of the system. A different nominating procedure in the future would thus require complementary mechanisms to attain the same objective through nonauthoritarian means.

The second trait of the political system was its ability to retain the loyalty of most of the country's politicians and organizational leaders. The system was governed by the principle that all politicians would be loyal to the system, and the system would be loyal to them. This principle was not just an effective instrument for exerting discipline over the party membership. It also served to nourish the expectation that one day, by adhering to party discipline, the individual would have his or her own chance to accede to power. In simple terms, political loyalty was exchanged for the expectation of future access to power and wealth (in many cases gained through corruption). The exceptional discipline of PRI members was based largely on the credible expectation that their loyalty would lead to privileges.

A third trait of the system was the importance of the unwritten rules of the political game. Mexico always has had plenty of written laws, regulations, and rules, but the unwritten rules have held sway. Paramount among these was the rule that the president was in charge. Those who failed to accept this were punished, usually through the imposition of a penalty associated with a formal rule. For example, a politician who failed to submit to a presidential nomination for a candidacy to a state government might have been charged with corruption. One thing had nothing to do with the other, but it was an effective way to maintain thorough control. Another important unwritten rule—and one that has been particularly costly to the PRI and its supporters during the recent years of reform—was access to corruption. Although most PRI politicians have engaged in or benefited from corrupt practices, virtually no one has been punished. Corruption was not a deviation from the system but one of its main traits.

The system that Calles invented was perfected by Lázaro Cárdenas, who created the so-called sectors—labor; the peasantry; popular groups; and, initially, the military. This political order was indeed exceptionally representative. It brought on board virtually all the relevant political groups of the time, so that most Mexicans felt represented by it. As a result, the PRI succeeded in drawing enough support to maintain social peace and foster economic development for much of the twentieth century.

The PRI's inner structure remained vital for many decades, but it could not keep pace with the changes that were overtaking society. Economic growth, rapid industrialization, urbanization, increasing levels of education, and the emergence of new interests contributed to an ever more complex society—one with values and interests that were different from those represented by the PRI. New political parties and organizations emerged and gained strength to the point at which, today, they have succeeded in mounting credible electoral challenges even for the presidency.

The mighty presidency of the 1930s remained at the core of the political system for sixty years, but it, too, has experienced the same erosion as other institutions. Just as the PRI's representativeness declined as society became more complex, the power of the presidency also waned. Occasionally a president would attempt to halt the relative decline in his powers by making use of actions or symbols that in the past had been successful means of enhancing his role; José López Portillo y Pacheco, for example, expropriated the banks in 1982 in a bid to reproduce the expropriation of the oil companies that had been so successful for Cárdenas in 1938. The results, of course, were devastating both for López Portillo and the economy.

Salinas recognized the growing weakness of the PRI and of the presidency—a recognition that led him to seek a different foundation for his own power. Rather than basing his government solely on control of the PRI and its members, Salinas organized a broad coalition of forces that included the marginally poor (mainly through his National Solidarity Program), the middle classes, the business community, and even the main opposition party, the PAN. By rejecting old taboos against building a closer relationship with the United States and the church or participating in international trade, he also drew substantial support from abroad. The coalition that he shaped became a formidable force during his term but ultimately failed to evolve into the kind of lasting political structure that might have helped avert the political downturn and economic crisis of 1994. Salinas never attempted to institutionalize the new coalition that he had built. The enhancement of presidential power that characterized his term began and ended with him. When he left office in 1994, he left unchanged the trend of weaker presidencies that had been under way for fifty years.

In the end, the economic reforms of the 1980s and 1990s proved to be insufficient to deal with Mexico's problems, even though they have indeed produced a strong economic rebound. The reforms were geared toward modernizing the system, not eliminating it; their ultimate aim was to maintain the political status quo. This inherent contradiction limited the potential success of reforms and, ultimately, produced the seeds of the debate that plagues Mexican politics today.

The nation's politics are evolving toward more ideological confrontation. Pro-reform constituencies consist mostly of the so-called renovators within the PRI (the group developed by Luis Donaldo Colosio, the murdered candidate for the presidency), the reformers in government, the pragmatists within the PAN, the business sector, various professional groups and associations, and much of the middle class. The anti-reform constituency has clustered around the PRD, the *dinos* (dinosaurs) in the PRI, the losers among the private sector, government unions (such as those for teachers and oil workers), and university students. While those on the pro-reform side advocate integrating Mexico into the world economy, accelerating liberalization, and developing institutions to deal with the ongoing political process, those in the anti-reform camp argue for immediate transfer of power, populism in the economy, and a thorough review of the policies on trade, privatization, and deregulation. The lines of conflict had been drawn by the time Ernesto Zedillo Ponce de León came into office late in 1994.

From the outset of his term, Zedillo redefined the role of the presidency as well as its objectives. Through his campaign and in his inaugural address, he insisted on three principles that broke with the decades-long tradition of presidential dominance. First, he argued that the rule of law, rather than unwritten rules, should guide Mexico's politics. Insisting that he would govern strictly according to the constitution, he relinquished extraconstitutional roles that had been adopted by all of his predecessors, such as leadership of the party and head of the nation's political class. Second, he called for sweeping reform of the judiciary and the Supreme Court. And third, he announced that he would maintain what he called a "healthy distance" from the PRI and would refrain from intervening in the selection of his successor as Mexican presidents before him had always done. Barely a week into his presidency, the Congress passed his judicial reform bill to create a much freer, more powerful, and uncorrupted Supreme Court, enabling it to act as a counterweight vis-à-vis the presidency.

Adopting the perspective of a citizen who had ended up in the presidential chair by chance rather than that of a political animal hungry for power, Zedillo identified a series of problems and abuses in the traditional structure of the presidency. By relinquishing those privileges not expressly cited in the constitution, he radically displaced the center of gravity of Mexican politics from the presidency to the political parties and the governors. Hence, even though Zedillo has retreated from many of his earlier positions, the "damage" done to the traditional "imperial" presidency cannot be undone.

Zedillo is not the first Mexican president to have argued for reform of the political system. Once in office, however, every previous would-be reformer had failed to deliver on his promises. In contrast, Zedillo has basically carried through on his commitment to reform. The consequences of this stance have ranged from the impressive to the ludicrous. Some state governors, used to taking their lead, if not their orders, from the president, have become paralyzed. Others have gone to the opposite extreme, acting as local bosses and organizing their administrations as if their states were independent entities. The Congress has become ever more active, far from the old rubber stamp mechanism that it used to be. It has been liberalized, undermining the old mechanisms of control and creating new spaces in which individuals can test the political waters and launch initiatives that would have been unthinkable only a few years ago. Members of Congress are no longer bound by authoritarian control but only by a very mild version of party discipline. About half the committee chairs in the Congress that ended in 1997 came from either the PRD or PAN (in contrast with none in the past), and bills initiated by the opposition have been presented, discussed, and voted on just as if they came from the PRI, something that never happened before. Opposition political parties, although benefiting from the new, more open climate, have experienced similar convulsions.

The PRI itself has also undergone radical change. The ultimate instrument of control within the party has traditionally been the monopoly held by the president over the selection of candidates for office and, above all, his successor. The *dedazo*, or "finger-pointing"—the name given to the process through which the president made his choices known—was the key source of his power. The president's monopoly on the final decision of who the candidate would be extended from the appointment of members of his cabinet (from which the presidential successor has emerged since the 1940s) to control over all candidacies for governorships and, frequently, congressional and other elected offices. The *dedazo* is associated with two other PRI institutions: a tradition of unanimity and the *tapado* (covered up). The *tapado*, a political institution since colonial times, was an additional element of control; nobody knew who the candidate would be and thus any one could be chosen, so everybody had to behave, just in case. The fact that aspiring politicians were not allowed to express their desire to become candidates was an important element of the system of discipline but also served as a means through which splits in the party were avoided. Since candidates did not express their aspirations overtly, none of the groups within the party needed to announce its preferences. Thus, the appearance of unanimity could be preserved in the final selection of the winner, and unnecessary bloodshed and public loss of face could be avoided. Although primitive, these procedures proved exceptionally effective decade after decade.

When Zedillo came into office, he was convinced of the need to change the system. It was not only his convictions that led him to this conclusion but also the fact that the PRI was experiencing greater difficulties in reaching intraparty consensus over the nomination of candidates and had even almost failed to win the very controversial presidential election in 1988. By announcing that he was relinquishing the right to name his successor and thus abandoning the presidential monopoly on power, however, Zedillo introduced a new factor of uncertainty into the PRI. For the first time in their history, members of the party were given the message that they needed to reform themselves and become competitive in an open electoral regime; the president would no longer stand for fraud or other illegal means to grab or maintain power. He would, Zedillo claimed, oversee a peaceful democratic evolution of the country's politics.

Members of the PRI had long been resentful of presidential abuses of power. Although such abuse had taken place for many years, resentment had grown in the 1980s as nonmilitant members of the party, many of them technocrats educated abroad, had been promoted to positions of power over longtime PRI members and as economic reforms (particularly deregulation and privatization) had greatly reduced the access of the party's hard core to traditional sources of wealth, usually through corruption. Zedillo's initial decision to distance himself from the party thus reinforced three important trends that had longer-term roots: growing electoral competition was making it ever more difficult for PRI members to have guaranteed access to power through elected offices; technical competence had become a formidable credential for political promotions, above party loyalty or active party membership; and economic reforms had reduced access to wealth through corruption. The increasing resentment of PRI activists reached its height at the party's 17th General Assembly (1996), when the hard core of party members adopted specific criteria that excluded most of the members of Zedillo's cabinet from the race for the PRI candidacy to the presidency or to governorships.

In changing the rules for the nomination of candidates, the party hard core was voicing the resentment of the old guard that had been displaced by the technocrats over the past two decades. Yet, the change was also evidence of the fact that the PRI's recent candidates no longer enjoyed wide support within the PRI or outside it, as their predecessors once did. The new rules do not strip the president of any potential influence in nominating a successor but do limit his options. Upon his inauguration, Zedillo announced that he would not appoint a successor because he recognized that open electoral competition makes such procedures irrelevant. In addition, his actions on other fronts have had the effect of diminishing the power of the presidency and, hence, of reducing his ability to actually drive, as his predecessors did, the process of succession. Since the succession process is such an important feature of the political system and such a critical component of traditional political controls, should Zedillo not appoint a successor (for whatever reason), he will have changed the system permanently. In so doing, he might open up new opportunities for electoral competition (and candidates for the PRI nomination could emerge from any area of the party), but he would also create a new political vacuum, since there would no longer be as credible and effective a control mechanism as the succession process itself used to be. This increasing irrelevance of traditional political processes is one more reason why hard-core institutions, such as the rule of law, have become so critical.

Zedillo's actions fundamentally altered the traditional structure of the Mexican presidency and, as a result, the broader political system. Throughout 1995, they led to accusations of weakness and calls for his resignation. Compared to presidents of fifty years ago, the current office of president is indeed weak, but this has less to do with the man himself than with the longer-term decline in the power of the Mexican presidency.

When Zedillo took office, there were two strategies through which he could have pursued his reform agenda. The first, which was supported by most politicians (and probably expected by most Mexicans), would have been to assume the traditional powers of the president and launch a thorough overhaul of the system from the top down. Those advocating this line of action expected a president who would use the powers of the office to transform the country by forcing change upon various constituencies, much as Salinas had done in the economic sphere. In other words, the president would have resorted to the same powers enjoyed by his predecessors but would have used them for a different purpose.

The alternative strategy—and the one adopted by Zedillo—followed the opposite course. Under this approach, the president abandoned the traditional powers of the presidency, thus forcing all other institutions, both new and old, to restructure. This course of action has compelled Mexico's other political actors to step into the vacuum created by the president's withdrawal. In fact, every realm that President Zedillo vacated was filled up by traditional members of the PRI and, in some cases, by members of the PRD, who are the only politicians savvy enough in the uses of power to take advantage of such an opportunity. Zedillo succeeded in reducing the powers of the presidency, of liberalizing Mexican politics further, and of creating a broader space for the development of competitive politics.

Yet, he also lost much of that power to the most reactionary, backward-looking strongholds of the old political system. By 1997, Zedillo had gone back full circle to the PRI, requiring its full-fledged commitment to sustain him in power and to make his economic policy sail through the Congress.

Most of the president's critics would rather have seen him pursue the first strategy. But the assumption on which that strategy is based is that democracy can be organized from above. By relinquishing the traditional—but unconstitutional—powers of the presidency, Zedillo has forced unprecedented change on Mexican society. In doing so, he has assumed the extraordinary risk that uncertainty will resolve itself within the boundaries of the law and the existing institutional framework. The hard core PRI members are among his strongest critics. Although many of them actually increased their political power, so did the opposition. Mexican politics, which has experienced growing liberalization for two decades now, was waiting for an opportunity, such as the one Zedillo created, to blossom. Although the PRI and PRD dinosaurs may have taken advantage of the withdrawal that Zedillo carried out, a good deal of political life today takes place in the media and in autonomous entities such as the Federal Electoral Institute, outside the control of the political parties or of the government. In that realm, the opposition, both the PRD and PAN, have a much better chance to have their views aired. Whatever the reality, PRI politicians perceive they have lost out.

Ultimately, a strong government is one that is effective at making and implementing decisions. The evidence to date suggests that Zedillo has been exceptionally strong in this respect. The longer-term question is whether the risks implicit in the president's strategy are manageable. Although the PRI maintains a large enough presence in the Congress elected in mid-1997 to pass legislation initiated by the administration, the absence of consensus on the future, particularly on economic policy, raises questions about these policies' permanence after the coming presidential election in 2000. To the extent that the economy improves the lot of a significant portion of Mexicans, the economic policy would become permanent, much as it did in Chile after Augusto Pinochet. The question is whether the improvement will be strong enough for it to have such an impact in a timely fashion. It is too early to tell whether this is the case, but one way to assess the odds is to examine the incentives that the president designed to enforce his policies and draw the broad range of political forces into his program.

Coping with Change

Constitutionally, the Mexican presidency is fairly weak. Its broad powers of old were the result of the peculiarities of the formation of the political system and tradition. As those real powers eroded over time, the power of the president began to be checked. But it was President Zedillo's decision to transform the political system that has accelerated the redefinition of the presidency and the political system as a whole. Although the system has experienced a lengthy process of liberalization since 1968 (mainly in growing electoral competition, ever greater opposition party presence, and an ever more open media), until now the formal structure of the system has remained untouched. Prior to this new wave of change, there have been many alterations within institutions and in the relationships among them. Yet, except for the opposition parties, all of the key players have remained the same. During Zedillo's term, for the first time since Calles invented the system, the players themselves began to change.

The traditional structure of the political system included, above all, the PRI and all of its associated and subordinated entities, including the labor federations and any number of clusters of people of all walks of life, plus the token participation of opposition parties. The new players in the process are not necessarily competing for power through elections, but they have become critical components of the process itself. Among these one can find an ever larger number of civic associations of all types (human rights, housing rights, antipoverty, environmental); private companies lobbying for their interests; a rapidly developing independent media that is neither tied to the old system of corruption nor dependent upon it for its survival; and checks imposed upon the political system by foreign entities and realities, from financial-market discipline to U.S. disputes about Mexicans' involvement in drugs. All of these factors play a growing role in Mexican politics.

Some of the recent changes have resulted from the president's own actions and, more importantly, from his early (but later rejected) decision to refrain from acting in some realms, notably within the PRI. Other changes derive from actual reforms implemented by the Zedillo administration, particularly in the realm of the judiciary and in the agreement on electoral reform reached in 1996. The agreement on electoral rules that was reached prior to the midterm elections of 1997 settled age-old disputes about the management of elections by creating an autonomous body on party and campaign financing, the Federal Electoral Institute; by fixing amounts of money that the government would transfer to each party in relation to the proportion of votes it received in the previous election; and by making the mayoralty of Mexico City an elected office. These agreements substantially advanced the creation of a level playing field for political parties to compete for votes. Even though there was no agreement on goals to be reached in the future, the parties did agree on the process to determine the way to get there: elections. The changing economic reality for most Mexicans, the result of an unconcluded reform but mainly of the badly mishandled devaluation of 1994, has also played an important role in shaping Mexicans' political attitudes. The question is how new institutions will be developed and whether they will succeed in meeting the objectives of representing society, channeling demands, promoting political participation, and maintaining stability. Despite the inherent difficulties of such a building process, there is some evidence that the gradual accumulation of practice, legislation, and enforcement will create new institutions, as the relatively new Supreme Court has shown.

The strategy launched by Zedillo had three components: to relinquish the unconstitutional powers of which his predecessors had made use; to strengthen key institutions, above all the judiciary and the legislature; and to adhere to the rule of law. Each of these elements would serve a specific purpose. Relinquishing the traditional but illegal powers of the presidency would force a restructuring of the political system by opening spheres of action to new political actors, as well as by redefining the role of old players. Strengthening the judiciary and the legislature was intended to introduce a credible and reliable dispute settlement mechanism, as well as to develop genuine checks and balances in the political system. Finally, adhering to the rule of law was meant to replace the unwritten rules of the game so as to make the system predictable for all political actors, rather than for members of the PRI alone. Zedillo launched initiatives—legal as well as political—in each of these realms, but halfway through his term, only some of them had either attained their goals or continued to be pursued. The judiciary experienced sweeping reforms, but the goal of introducing the rule of law was done away with altogether. However, President Zedillo has not attempted to recover the old powers of the presidency, even though he ended up as close to the PRI as any, of his predecessors. In fact, getting close ultimately entailed not prosecuting the old guard of the party and, therefore, was incompatible with the pursuit of the rule of law.

Once it became clear that the president intended to relinquish sweeping powers, the system began to unravel. The process happened over a period of time but culminated in the PRI's 17th General Assembly when the party took over many of the powers relinquished by the president, above all the control of the party apparatus and the presidential succession process. By relinquishing control of the party, Zedillo unleashed forces within the PRI that ultimately came to demand more power and control for themselves. This may not mean too much in a political system in which the PRI is ever less in charge, but it does alter the underpinning factors of control and stability in the system. To the extent that the president loses control of the succession process (which the new party rules limit but do not eliminate), the political system will end up facing a new set of questions and challenges, all related to the complex process of its political maturation. Although the president had second thoughts about his original plan to maintain a healthy distance from the party, once the monopoly of presidential power within the PRI was broken up, it vanished completely into the hands of the party's most skillful members, usually those of the old guard.

Something similar has taken place in the judiciary, where the Supreme Court has taken strong stands on issues that traditionally were central concerns of the presidency. Virtually all of the court's rulings on the constitutionality of laws have been initiated as a result of disputes among politicians from various government entities. This is partly the result of the fact that individuals are barred from addressing the Supreme Court directly (only the state and federal governments, as well as a minimum of 30 percent of the federal Congress, are allowed to bring cases to the court), but it also indicates that disputes that in the past were settled by one man's decision are today being settled openly in court. The legislature, too, has experienced profound change, largely due to the increasingly active participation by congressional members from opposition parties. In a word, the members of the PRI have been the first ones to resort to the courts to settle disputes, which may signal that they will abandon illegal and fraudulent procedures in favor of legal ones.

The more complex issue of the rule of law is not yet resolved, however. The president's goal has been to create a predictable environment, rather than actually to develop a system based on the rule of law. The emphasis on the law is meant to compel government officials and society overall to follow the letter of the law. However, laws can be changed, and rules can be adopted by the government unilaterally. Thus, as long as written rules are abided by, there is compliance with the law. This is not the same as the rule of law, which is meant to protect the individual from the arbitrary actions of the government, but it represents significant progress over the dominance of unwritten rules in Mexican society. Although rules are now written and not informal, Mexico still lives under the rule of rule rather than the rule of law. And the difference is not subtle: one entails sticking to what the rules say but retaining the ability to change those rules at any point in time and with utter disregard for due process. The rule of law stems from a totally different premise: the law has to protect the individual from the arbitrariness of the government, which means sticking to the rules but also not doing anything that could harm the individual. The government's concept of the law falls short of the latter for two reasons. First, the government still retains extraordinary powers to decide upon and alter rules at any point and before everyone else, and second, the government seeks certainty, not the rule of law. The end result is that certainty becomes elusive since it depends upon the will of a party or faction in power. To the extent that there are no checks and balances that limit the ability of a government (or the party with a majority in the Congress) to change the law, certainty becomes strictly tied to individuals.

It is relatively easy for governments to settle on desirable goals and government objectives that are often unimpeachable in wording and intent, but what governments actually do has a far greater effect on citizens than what they say. By its actions a government creates incentives that determine the way society responds. When a government is consistent, society is likely to respond consistently. When it provides incentives for institutional responses, these are what it will get. The Zedillo administration, following in the steps of its predecessor, has been extraordinarily equivocal in the incentives it has provided to society, and not surprisingly, the response of society is far from clear.

There are many examples of the government's ambivalent signals regarding institutional reform. During the Salinas administration, the federal government often condoned electoral fraud, then conceded defeat in postelectoral negotiations (as in the case of the state of Guanajuato in 1991). By agreeing to negotiate "under the table" following an election, the administration provided an incentive for opposition parties to concentrate their actions not on the electoral race itself but on raising doubts about its outcome. When opposition parties learned that the way to obtain a role in government lay not in open electoral competition but in postelection negotiations, they pursued this path. Like many other groups in Mexican society, they were acting rationally in response to government incentives.

Mexico faces plenty of challenges in the political realm. Some of these stem from deteriorating realities, whereas others come from rising (or dashed) expectations. Most, however, arise from the fact that the country's judiciary has been so corrupt and inept that it has failed to fulfill its role of settling disputes. On top of that, the politicization of judicial decisions and the unpredictable behavior of government have provided incentives for groups to rebel rather than to seek relief through the courts. For example, after the government agreed to the demands of the Zapatista Army of National Liberation (EZLN), the Popular Revolutionary Army (EPR) made its appearance in 1995 to seek similar concessions. The Zapatistas, who had rebelled January 1, 1994, were able to manipulate Mexican politics and politicians for two years and got extraordinary concessions (as yet unratified) from the government that go as far as to create autonomous regions in the country.

Something similar has taken place in the government's dealing with unions. For over twenty years, for example, the government negotiated exclusively with the national teachers' union, despite the fact that there were many splinter groups. Such a strategy maintained the lid on autonomous movements and on the possibility that some sections of the union might move on to other parties. From the government's perspective, negotiating with one single entity was a politically important objective. Altering that strategy might have been a way to decentralize power, to introduce competition into the union, or even to split the union for whatever purposes. Nothing as ambitious as that has been part of the government's tactics. Yet, in 1996 it abandoned its policy of not negotiating with the National Coordinator of Teachers (CNM), one of the more radical, PRD-leaning, splinter organizations. It did so because of that group's very visible, disruptive, and successful demonstrations in Mexico City. The government ended up subordinating its general policies to the interests of a pressure group. And in a similar action closely tied to these events, the president fired the chief of police of Mexico City because of the calls of demonstrators.

In all of these cases, the government sends the message that it will negotiate with anyone who demonstrates, which only leads to many more demonstrations. For example, early in the Zedillo administration, the municipal president of Ciudad Juárez organized a blockade of the main bridge across the border with the United States in order to collect a toll for the city. After several days, the federal government agreed to transfer 10 percent of the revenues of the bridge to the city. This agreement was tantamount to a license to block every other bridge or toll road in the country, and not surprisingly, more blockades followed. In such a context, the government ends up not much more than a hostage of special interests that, regardless of their representativeness (or lack thereof), can exercise a disproportionate amount of power.

There may be occasions when negotiation is the only possible solution. Although many in Mexico advocate equal and consistent application of law, there are areas of Mexican society that do not lend themselves to clear-cut solutions. When the subject is, for example, a real or alleged Indian uprising, enforcing the law might mean thousands of deaths, a possibility that would lead virtually any government to negotiate. But negotiating outside the boundaries of the laws that the government is committed to upholding and enforcing ends up providing strong incentives for future rebellions. The government's message becomes even more ambiguous when compliance with the law has been that government's top priority, as with the current administration. The result is that, for the past several years, two successive administrations pursuing almost opposite rationales—one for the rule of law, the other for the maintenance of the status quo—have ended up undermining their own credibility, and there is little prospect for it to be regained.

There is, of course, another side to the story. Groups within Mexican society that have made it their goal to alter the status quo have the incentive to challenge the government at every turn. The use of passive resistance as a means to transform the established order has long been known to be an effective weapon for political ends. When such groups, from the PRD to the EZLN, from the teachers' union to human rights organizations, and even disaffected PRI clusters (including those that refuse to accept the new terms of competition for access to power), purposefully enact such a strategy and are met by a government willing to break its own rules, the picture is complete. The established order is altered by passive resistance rather than through established procedures, and a new incentive has been created that makes future efforts to strengthen institutions even less likely to succeed. Changing the status quo is obviously a worthy objective in such a polarized, poverty-stricken society. However, not having credible and predictable rules and procedures is dangerous, for it breeds violence and instability.

Mexico's governance since the student movement of 1968 has largely been one of exceptions. There has been no long-term strategy in the political realm, only reaction. This has produced the incentives exemplified previously, but also some more dangerous decisions. The management of key issues, such as personal security in the country's large cities as well as those related to drugs and drug trafficking, has led to the ever larger involvement of the military in domestic politics. Its involvement has been the result of desperation more than of strategy. The notion that the military, being relatively isolated and independent from daily politics, can be immune from corruption, has led the government to rely on it to an increasing extent. The military has long been involved in the war against drug trafficking and recently has been given charge of the police forces of most large towns, including Mexico City. By participating in the management of the country, the military has also become much more aware of the complexities and risks involved in government. Yet, it has also come in contact with many sources of corruption and has found it extremely difficult to resolve problems as complex as those facing police forces in major cities. This complexity has probably cured it of a desire for further involvement in politics, but the benefits some of its members have come to enjoy will undoubtedly turn them into permanent participants in the country's governance. The result is not the militarization of politics but the potential corruption of the military that may emanate from this additional failing of the country's political process.

It is in this context that the July 1996 National Political Agreement on Electoral Reform, accepted by all political parties and the government and passed unanimously by Congress, constituted an extraordinary accomplishment. Not only did all of Mexico's parties join in the agreement, but by doing so they agreed implicitly to abandon passive resistance and other extrainstitutional tactics and follow the course of electoral competition. Although the substance of the electoral agreement may not be overly ambitious, for it largely made into law what had already been accepted in practice such as the independence of the electoral commission, its symbolic impact is enormous. The agreement is not likely to eliminate all government incentives for extrainstitutional action, but it does diminish the likelihood that political parties will return to such tactics. (It does little, however, to prevent local governments, unions, or potential guerrilla movements from doing so.) The unanimous passing of the electoral law was seen by the parties and presented by the president as the foundation of a new political order that all major political actors had participated in and thus were bound by, including the agreements spelled out within it. In the future, any dispute—or attempted coup—could always be referred back to the initial agreement (which in Spain proved critical in settling the attempted military takeover in 1979). Thus it was unfortunate that when the time came to pass legislation implementing the agreement, the PRI and the president decided to trash the consensus that had been reached at the constitu-

tional level, by not including in the law eighteen specific under-
standings among the parties. None of them was critical to democracy, but the notion of consensus was indeed wounded.

In sum, the Zedillo administration introduced a strategy to deal
with Mexico's political ills that, in theory, represents a radical departure from previous policy. This has led to dramatic transformations
in some of the most critical relationships that lie at the core of the
political system, such as the one between the president and the PRI;
it has strengthened the judiciary and encouraged an increasingly
active legislature; and it has begun to bring the main opposition parties into the political system. These are significant accomplishments.
They will not be sufficient, however, to alter Mexico's political system as long as the incentive structure preserves extrainstitutional
remedies as viable and rational courses of action.

The New Political Arena

The current uncertainty that permeates Mexican society springs
from many sources. An important factor is the emergence of an
increasingly active polity made up of opposition parties, nongovernmental organizations, unions, and organized interests of all kinds.
Behind this explosion of political action is a lack of credible institutional structures; an absence of consensus over what constitute the
rules of the game; and the damaged credibility of the government. In
addition, the economic depression experienced by most Mexicans in
1995 and 1996 has further undermined government credibility and
fueled the strength of opposition parties. The "old" political system
consisted of a series of institutions that maintained control, nurtured
the appearance of consensus, and provided minimum access to
power to those that played successfully within the PRI. A rapidly
changing society such as that of Mexico today requires different
institutions. Some of them are beginning to emerge, such as a fairly
independent Supreme Court and the Federal Electoral Institute, but
as important as these are, they are insufficient to channel demands
from the population and to settle disputes. Mexican congressional
representatives do not have any incentive to represent their con-
stituents, since there is no reelection; hence, they serve their party's
interests, the government's, or their own. The lack of rule of law
impedes the development of independent unions or, for that matter,
of new investments. More important, the lack of checks and balances
creates an environment in which there are no limits to how much
damage a party or government can do when in office.

But these domestic factors are not the only sources of uncertainty for Mexico. To a large extent, they are merely reflections of what is happening elsewhere in the world. The visibility of Mexican politics and corruption in the foreign media and, particularly, in the United States has become the foremost source of pressure on the government. The visibility of U.S. politics and elections in the Mexican media (now enhanced by broadcasts direct from satellite, outside the realm of control of any local authority) makes it difficult for Mexicans to ignore the comparison of the two political systems. In 1994, Mexico's presidential candidates held a pre-election debate for the first time in Mexican history, and such debates now have become a staple of most races. U.S. labor unions, the staunchest opponents of NAFTA, have shifted their energies from opposing free trade to joining forces with their counterparts in Mexico to enhance their power within Mexican society. New technologies such as the Internet, an increasingly active media, transnational coalitions of all sorts, and foreign criticism all play a significant role in shaping the nature of Mexico's current transformation. The examples of these are endless, but they are particularly obvious in the areas of human rights, labor, the environment, and the media.

Perhaps above all, it is global change that makes Mexico's transformation inevitable. The globalization not only of production but also of values and institutions is having a dramatic impact on Mexico, whether or not Mexicans and their leaders are ready for it. The key question for Mexico today is whether it can cope with the onslaught of change. Does it have, or can it develop, the ability to build political institutions that can withstand the impact of these new realities?

Whether or not Mexico learns to cope with the unprecedented level of change under way, its consequences are already evident. The explosion of information is not just a quantitative phenomenon having to do with the fact that there are many more sources of information available to Mexicans. The Mexican media is experiencing an impressive qualitative transformation as well. Denunciation of corruption, a dangerous pursuit in the past (as the killings of literally hundreds of reporters over the years can attest), has become a daily phenomenon. Exposés of unlawful as well as legal but potentially improper deals between the private sector and the government have become the staple of newspapers and magazines. Opinion polls, carried out by professionals, have become indispensable tools for analysis as well as for government decisionmaking. The newly active media—which had been growing for several years after *Proceso*, a weekly magazine, was launched in 1976 and was boosted up by the inauguration of *Reforma*, a daily in Mexico City—have been criticized for pursuing impact over accuracy. Although some of this criticism is legitimate, the important point is that after decades of censorship, both implicit and explicit, the media have become a political factor to be reckoned with. Furthermore, public demand for the information, opinions, and polls provided by the media is well entrenched. All these developments go a long way toward diminishing the effectiveness and legitimacy of the government in monopolizing or manipulating events.

Political Parties

Mexican voters will now have a chance to compare the programs and candidates presented to them by the various political parties in a fairly balanced fashion. All parties have equal access to the media, and their funding is secure. But despite the attempts of all parties to present a moderate face, not all of them stand for the same principles and objectives.

The PRI is the most difficult party to define and characterize because it has been a political system in its own right. All ideological and political currents are present within the PRI, but historically, it has been a party on the center left, advocating policies based, organized, and led by the government. Deeply ingrained in the PRI philosophy is the Rousseauian notion that the state is more than the sum of the collective and that, therefore, the bureaucracy can and should establish the path of development and the limits on individual action and individual freedom. The latter notwithstanding, it has been a series of three PRI administrations that has led the country through the deepest economic reforms the country has ever seen. These reforms have stripped the government of many of its properties, including steel, telephones, and some petrochemicals, and reduced the power of the bureaucracy through privatizations and deregulation of the economy. In a way, the PRI's difficulties with the electorate have to do with the fact that the party personifies both the past and the present, even when these are totally opposite in character.

The PAN is a party of the right that has moderated its ideological extremes over the years. It was born as a reaction to the PRI (then the Party of the Mexican Revolution) in 1939, and was shaped to resemble the right-wing European parties of the era. These European parties underwent profound transformations after World War II and emerged as modern Christian Democratic parties, but the PAN did not. Hence, the PAN embodies many of those contradictions today: its closeness with the church, its social policies (against abortion, miniskirts, and the like), and its small capitalism (as opposed to market economics). In contrast with the PRI and PRD, the PAN is a collection of regional parties rather than a national organization. Each of those regions has a different constituency, which explains many of the stark contrasts one can find inside the PAN: there are free marketers living next to protectionists and secular politicians next to members of the clergy.

The PRD is an odd mix of PRI defectors and a collection of left-wing parties, from the Mexican Communist Party to the Trotskyites. Its philosophy reflects its origins: it has attempted to mix hard left, Marxist politics with a lighter version of the statist philosophy inherited from the left wing of the PRI. The PRD grew out of a coalition organized by the so-called Democratic Current inside the PRI that quit the party after Cuauhtémoc Cárdenas failed to get the PRI nomination for candidate to the presidency in 1988. Cárdenas then ran as candidate of the National Democratic Front, which eventually became the basis of the alliance that founded the PRD. This party of the left has been striving to gain the votes of disaffected citizens. Its economic program has been changing constantly in an effort to appeal to those voters who have suffered from the country's economic reforms. It has greatly benefited from the endless conflict between Ernesto Zedillo and Carlos Salinas, which has left Cárdenas, the PRD boss, with credibility as someone who has opposed them both.

The theoretical alternatives available to Mexican voters are quite clear. Though the parties have, as yet, proven to be incapable of arguing for programs and debating the issues, their positions are becoming more obvious to voters as time goes by. Each of these parties embodies a radically different view of the world, and their constituencies tend to be very different. The PRI is a party based upon the Mexico at the time the party was created: peasants, marginalized people, and the urban poor. The party—as opposed to some of its members, like Salinas—has found it very difficult to develop strong constituencies within the middle classes. The PRI has, since the reforms began, been able to count on the support of the modern sectors of the economy and the country's prime business people. The PAN's constituency is typically middle class and urban. Its contingents include the largest number of professionals of any party. The PRD, however, has a mixed constituency: it is largely an urban party, with support among voters in the lower middle classes, typically in the old industrial areas, who have lost out economically in recent times. In contrast with the PAN, which has a large base of support throughout the country, the PRD's constituencies are located in and around Mexico City. In addition to its urban contingents, the PRD has solid rural support in the states of Guerrero, Morelos, and Oaxaca.

The party structure of the country reflects the old correlation of forces. It is conceivable that the whole party structure could be altered, should the PRI lose an election, particularly at the presidential level. A PRI loss could easily lead to both a profound reform of the party itself, much as happened to the communist parties of Eastern Europe after the fall of the Berlin Wall in 1989, as well as to a split in the party ranks. The reform of the party might create a competitive party that could eventually regain power once again. The splits that might take place could reshape the whole party structure. Members of the PRI left, for example, might negotiate a merger with the PRD. The opposite possibility—members of the PRI right merging with the PAN—looks less likely largely because of the very different nature of those entities. Yet, Mexico could end up with a modern party structure with parties on the left, on the right, and in the center, but all of them pretty well demarcated and defined—which is not the case today.

The Complex Transition Ahead

Today, "transition" is one of the most widely abused terms in Mexico's political debate. The difficulty is that a clear notion of transition implies that there is both a point of departure and a place of arrival. The term was coined to encapsulate the political process in Spain, where an enviably orderly transition of power took place following the death of Francisco Franco that led to the consolidation of democracy, the adoption of a new constitution, and the defeat of an attempted coup. The context of the Spanish transition was radically different. To begin with, Franco himself had spent almost two decades shaping the institutions that would inherit from him the functions of government. In addition, the new regime was easy to distinguish from the old. Neither of these circumstances characterizes Mexico today. The issue is critical for Mexico: the PAN and PRD have signed on to the process of change through elections because they expect to reap direct benefits in the form of electoral victories. If the PRI were to win a clean and fair election, as it may very well do in the year 2000, the opposition parties may not be willing to recognize the results, posing a crucial dilemma for the nascent democracy. The PRI has dominated Mexican politics for so long and is associated with so many vices that without alternation of parties in power, democracy would be left wanting. Ultimately, this goes to the core of

Mexico's complex political moment: elections are a component of democracy but not its only feature; the PRI may very well dominate the electoral process in this new era, but that would not by itself bring about democracy and all of its components. New institutions are in their infancy, and the old system persists even as the new one is emerging. Moreover, there is no consensus on what the future should look like. This is why the key to Mexico's political evolution lies in the accumulation of agreements on procedures, such as the recent electoral law, and on incremental successes by parties that today are in opposition, so that all build an allegiance to an institutional, as opposed to violent, way of settling disputes. To the extent that political parties and other interested groups are able to agree on procedures, they will be able to shape the future one step at a time.

An important question in this regard is whether the two significant parties that today are in the opposition (PAN and PRD) have the skills to govern. The PAN was created in 1939 and has a long list of cadres that have spent literally decades in the Congress (if one adds all the years they have been in the legislature). The party today governs six states and about 40 percent of all Mexicans at the municipal level. Though the party has national presence, it is really a party of regions, each of which has a different ideological stance. As in any party, there are religious zealots as well as liberal intellectuals in the PAN. The party platform resembles that of a traditional Christian social democratic party, with important cleavages on issues such as abortion, family, relations with the United States, foreign trade, and the economy in general. The party is not, as is often assumed, committed to a market economy, although it does espouse some of its features. The PAN is strong in the big cities; in the north and west of the country; and in several specific states such as Puebla, Guanajuato, and Yucatán. As it gains experience at governing at the local level, the PAN will become a credible alternative to the PRI.

The PRD is largely run by former members of the PRI, but its ideological commitments reflect its hard-core radical left. It stands for relative isolation in economic matters; for an active government in procuring benefits for the poor and the unemployed; and for an "independent" foreign policy, which means greater political distance from the United States. The former PRI members in the PRD usually have long experience in governing and are extremely skillful politically. The PRD's strengths are in the south and center of Mexico, where it has developed a formidable political machine. Both the PAN and PRD stand for very different objectives, but both have learned how to portray themselves before the public as credible and moderate alternatives to the PRI. However, every time they have a chance, they evidence their commitment to deeper, more ideological differences vis-à-vis the PRI.

The political transition that Mexico has embarked upon will be successful to the extent that all the participating parties and the government can stick to procedures and find more benefits in doing so than in attempting to take a noninstitutional or violent route. In this, the government's actions will set precedents. The initial political agenda of the Zedillo administration was extremely broad. It included federalism; freedom of expression and the media; relations among the executive, judicial, and legislative branches of government; and the provision of political rights. There were holes in this agenda, particularly in the area of the rule of law, but it was sweeping nonetheless. This agenda set the tone for negotiations among the political parties, and when it was launched, members of the PAN enthusiastically joined the process, whereas those of the PRD remained on the sidelines. The president probably assumed he would be able to bring the PRI into the negotiations without much difficulty. As time went by, however, it became obvious that the members of the PRI had an agenda of their own and would not cave in easily. By the 1997 midterm elections, the only thing the parties had been able to agree on was on electoral reform, which the Congress passed. Everything else was left unfinished. At the root of the uncertainty that characterizes Mexico today are the consequences of failing to address the entire agenda. Electoral reforms addressed the issues of concern to the political parties and, as a result, they were essentially satisfied with the results; but the issues of concern to the average man or woman in the street were left out. In this context, the possibility of parties alternating in power does not have the balancing impact that it would otherwise have but rather the opposite: it creates extraordinary uncertainty.

Over time, it may be possible for a new political agenda to gain momentum. At this time all that can be done is to speculate about the potential implications of a revival of negotiations. One way to assess the potential for Mexico's successful transformation is to assume, for the sake of argument, that the entire agenda proposed by the government is agreed upon by the parties and passed into law. If this were to be accomplished, the political process would be strengthened, but would Mexico's problems be resolved? Of course, the very existence of consensus among all of the political parties on crucial issues that the country is facing—such as elections, the economy, and NAFTA—would remove many of the obstacles that today hinder Mexico's rapid economic recovery by fostering an increase in private savings and investment. But for that consensus to emerge, it has to be compatible with the objective needs of the economy. If, for example, such a consensus were formed in opposition to the government's economic policy—not an altogether unlikely scenario—it would end up being counterproductive. As has been argued, most Mexicans have yet to benefit from the reforms of the past decade; for them, the "new" economy has not spelled relief, higher incomes, or more jobs. In this context, developing a consensus against an economic policy aimed at actively participating in the global economy would be a fairly easy feat. For this reason, neither the PRD nor the left of the PRI have been willing to go beyond rhetoric in criticizing the economic policy of the government. In other words, everybody, from the government to the last of the opposition parties, is hoping that the economy will improve the lot of Mexicans soon enough to avoid the need to articulate a position against the core of the economic policy. Obviously, members of the PRI hope that success will come earlier rather than later, and the opposite would be preferred by the parties in opposition. This issue will undoubtedly underlie the political campaigns for the presidential race in the year 2000.

To the extent that the country has no alternative but to participate actively in world markets, its options for development and its potential for generating wealth will multiply. But Mexico will only accomplish its economic goals when it eliminates the current sources of uncertainty, of which the lack of rule of law is paramount. Political agreements among parties are a necessary condition for economic development in Mexico today, but they are no substitute for the rule of law.

The 1997 Elections

The 1997 elections took place at a particularly relevant moment in Mexico's modern history, for they happened soon after the economic collapse of 1995, which not only caused havoc in the international financial markets but also led to a dramatic decline in incomes for most Mexicans. In addition to this, there has always been the presumption among many Mexicans that the PRI has maintained a monopoly in Mexican politics largely due to systematic electoral fraud. Since these elections were held on the basis of electoral legislation that was passed unanimously in the Congress, all political actors were expecting major developments. At stake were six state governorships plus, for the first time in modern history, the direct election of a mayor for Mexico City. Also, there were elections for all of the lower house of Congress, one-fourth of the Senate, and many local governments. The two key races were those of Mexico City, a very visible political position, and the Congress, which has to approve all legislation and, particularly, the yearly public budget.

The election results were equivalent to an earthquake. The PRD, in the person of Cuauhtémoc Cárdenas, won the mayoralty of Mexico City by a large margin; the PAN added two more state governors (for a total of six); and, most important, the PRI lost control of the Congress. Each of these changes entails a break with the past. Though the PAN was already governing four other states, this time it was able to swallow two of the wealthiest and fastest growing ones, Nuevo León and Querétaro.

The most dramatic change undoubtedly came in Mexico City and the federal Congress. Mexico City's mayoralty in the hands of a party other than the PRI raises questions about conflict at several levels. First and foremost, the city, traditionally controlled directly by the federal government, will now have to define its limits vis-à-vis the federal government on issues as simple but critical as whether the federal government should pay property taxes or pay for its water use. By the same token, the complexity of a city with the size and problems of Mexico's capital will test Cárdenas's skills and competence. Much more important, however, the visibility of the Mexico City mayor will turn him into the second most important politician in the nation. The victory of Cuauhtémoc Cárdenas signals open competition for the presidency in the year 2000, something that has never happened in modern Mexico.

Similarly, the loss of the PRI's majority in the Congress opens up a radically new scenario for Mexican politics. The lack of an absolute majority brings into question the ability of the legislature to enact laws, particularly those that have to be passed for the government to work and function, such as each year's budget. The new congressional reality is that the parties, plus the government, will now have to negotiate among themselves rather than bear the yoke of the PRI and the administration. Some bills will pass, but others will not. The government technocrats will have to learn to compromise without affecting the core of their economic program. In other words, Mexico's government will become as complex and diverse as those of most other states. What makes this process particularly difficult is the fact that the country is entering into an era of democratic politics without a consolidated economy. Undoubtedly, the ongoing shifts in Mexican politics evidence the growing maturity of Mexican voters and their willingness to carry out a gradual and institutional (as opposed to violent) transformation of the nation's politics.

As the elections proved, electoral politics have become truly competitive. Access to the media was equitable, and all parties enjoyed government financing of their campaigns. The PRD ended up being the only party with a clear, sensible, and ultimately successful strategy. The PAN and PRI proved to be incapable of understanding the shift in voters' preferences and concerns, particularly in the geographic center of the nation (Mexico City, the states of Mexico, Guerrero, and Michoacán, etc.). The election results create the opportunity to begin to develop checks and balances because power will now be divided among the parties. But they also pose serious dilemmas for a fairly undeveloped political system. This marks a new reality for Mexican politics and raises the question of whether the appropriate institutions exist in order to cope with the new reality. The fact is, however, that Mexicans were fed up with the rule of the PRI, with continuous economic crises, and with corruption. Exit polls revealed that as much as 50 percent of the vote for the PRD and for the PAN was a vote of protest. Hence, as politics gears up toward the presidential race of 2000, the big question is which party will be able to earn the confidence of the 30–40 percent of voters that have no party allegiance and that in both 1994 and 1997 determined the result of the elections.

The Future of Mexican Politics

Probably the most positive sign at the moment is that Mexico's political extremes continue to narrow. Although a few months ago the positions of some of the main political actors encompassed policies that could be considered radical, such as support for guerrilla action, these positions have been abandoned and the extremes of the parties moderated. In fact, at times it appears that, although the political arena will not be free of conflict, Mexico's parties will share sufficient common ground to keep conflict and its negative consequences to a minimum. In this respect, the gradual institutionalization of the political parties is good news, even if the process ahead will be complex.

Despite the ups and downs that inevitably will ensue regarding the influence of inexperienced parties and politicians in government, as well as challenges to the authority of the government, there are two reasons to be optimistic. The first reason is that government and politics are increasingly less relevant for Mexico's political and economic actors. The government's excessive powers have not been completely eliminated, but it is less able than in the past to act arbitrarily. This is evident in both the economic realm, where successful firms and corporations are today freer from government influence than they were in the past (when, for example, they had to get the

bureaucracy to sanction virtually any decision or to grant them permits, subsidies, concessions, and so on), and in the political arena,
where freedom of expression continues to grow. This was also evident on election day in 1994, when 78 percent of registered voters
showed up to vote, in comparison with a historical average of 55
percent, signaling that Mexicans will not tolerate violent or other
noninstitutional forms of political change. The other reason to be
optimistic is that Mexicans appear to stand solidly behind an institutional outcome. In a recent poll, Mexicans agreed overwhelmingly
on three points: they abhor the government, they are skeptical of the
opposition, and they reject violence. The key to the future may well
lie in this simple but extraordinarily powerful mix of values and per-
ceptions. Mexicans realize that the PRI represents invaluable experience relative to the other parties, but they have been abused so long
by the PRI governments that they are willing to try any alternative
that is not committed to violence. In a way, the poll results may signal Mexicans' desire to scare the PRI into changing its ways, know-
ing full well that either the PRD or the PAN can serve as vehicles to
attain that objective. It may also reflect a very mature electorate, one
that is fully aware of the challenges that lie ahead and of the frailty
of existing political institutions.

Will Mexico face political upheaval in the future? This may be
the wrong question. Mexicans do not want violence, nor do they
seem likely to support violent confrontations in the future. Mexico's
political ills are of a different nature. On the one hand, they have to
do with institutionalizing political conflict, an area in which great
progress already has been made, as evidenced by the electoral law.
However, if any mishap does occur, the odds are that it will take
place in the electoral realm. The emergence of the EPR, for example,
shows that existing institutions are far from capable of handling all
of the challenges facing Mexico today and that the government is far
from being able to design a long-term strategy to deal with such
challenges. On the other hand, from a political perspective, the ability of the economy to recover and experience high rates of growth
rests fundamentally on the governments ability to bring about the
rule of law. Without it, uncertainty will be too high for Mexico to
succeed in world markets.

2

Crisis and Economic Change in Mexico

Mauricio A. González Gómez

For the last twenty-five years, during four presidential administrations, Mexico has experimented with various economic development models with only questionable success. In the 1970s and early 1980s the government increased its intervention in the economy through higher federal spending, a larger number of public sector firms that were directly involved in economic activity, laws oriented to controlling the behavior of different markets—particularly their prices or outputs—and barriers to foreign competition such as import tariffs or quotas designed to protect Mexican producers from their foreign counterparts. In the late 1980s and early 1990s the opposite strategy was followed. It aimed to correct the imbalances produced by the so-called mixed economy (the combination of direct government intervention and private economic involvement). It began by reducing the size of government (i.e., the number of public sector employees and federal agencies, investment projects, and, in particular, the oversized public sector debt). At the same time, the private sector was given greater freedom to function in different markets. Free market policies were applied in the financial and agricultural sectors, as well as in some key areas of the manufacturing and service sectors. These policies were complemented by strong trade liberalization efforts aimed at promoting Mexican exports and reducing the cost of imported goods and services in an effort to make Mexico's economy more globally competitive. In spite of this intense process of economic transformation (especially between 1984 and 1994), each of the last four presidential administrations has ended with an economic crisis: Echeverría in 1976, López Portillo in 1982, de la Madrid in 1987, and Salinas in 1994.

For most international observers, the economic changes implemented by President Carlos Salinas de Gortari and his highly trained economic team of young technocrats (most of whom were in their thirties and early forties) seemed capable of producing a stable, high-growth economy that would eventually improve the well-being of most Mexicans. For the first time in many years, there was high, stable, and continuous economic growth. Nevertheless, the economic strategy could not prevent the peso devaluation and economic crisis of December 1994. Many elements were in place to ensure economic stability: a balanced budget, a free trade agreement with the largest economy in the world, an autonomous central bank that could enforce a monetary policy independent of political pressures, and renewed economic growth with increasing real wages and employment. Unfortunately, a combination of neglect, arrogance, and the absence of timely decisions by the government and other social actors led to crisis instead of success. Was the crisis an unavoidable consequence of Mexico's economic reforms, or was it caused by mismanagement and overconfidence on the part of public sector officials? Without a clear understanding of the causes and consequences of the 1994–1995 economic crisis, Mexico runs the risk of repeating its earlier mistakes.

In addition, earlier economic crises ultimately brought about important and lasting reforms that otherwise might not have been implemented. Examples include the public expenditure reduction plan initiated in 1983; the trade liberalization process introduced in 1985, which led to a variety of free trade agreements, including the North American Free Trade Agreement (NAFTA); the financial sector liberalization of 1987; and the tax and fiscal reforms of 1989. The aftermath of the 1994–1995 peso crisis also produced some economic reforms. Most of them continued previous trends: the privatization of public services, including ports, railroads, airports, and telecommunications, as well as increased government deregulation in the form of fewer permits and licenses for business operations. Social security was also drastically reformed after the 1994 crisis through the introduction of a private pension fund system designed to promote private savings.

Despite these developments, however, in the first half of President Ernesto Zedillo Ponce de León's administration (1994–1997), government efforts have focused on overcoming short-term problems caused by the crisis rather than on laying the foundation for improved economic development, which includes not only a restoration of previous levels of growth but also a better distribution of the benefits of that growth.

Debate over the development strategy that best suits Mexico has been rare even among those sectors that should be most interested, such as the government, the private sector, academic institutions, and political parties. It is not clear whether this relative lack of interest is real or whether it results from authoritarian rule that stifles more active participation by groups in Mexican society. Official statements about economic development are themselves ambiguous. Leaning for the most part toward support for the free market, they nonetheless exhibit some reservations. Given this situation, it may be more accurate to describe Mexico's economic development strategy as incomplete. Its lack of continuity, efficacy, and decisiveness is evident in the areas of agrarian reform, where expected benefits have not materialized; education and training policies, which have failed to adequately improve the skills of the population; and labor reforms, particularly those intended to increase productivity, which are still pending. The need for a strong and clear economic development strategy is made even more acute by the fact that Mexico faces strong competition in the new global economy from other countries in Latin America, from Eastern Europe, and from Asia.

Mexico's poorly defined economic strategy has led to a poorly integrated productive apparatus and to problems of a lack of economic concentration in certain sectors and regions. For example, between 1995 and 1997, economic performance in the export sector has been far more impressive than performance in the domestic sector. Real exports increased 53 percent during 1995–1996, whereas internal production for the domestic market diminished by 8 percent. The domestic economy, however, represents about 70 percent of total activity. It includes the majority of firms and generates the most employment. The gap between export and domestic performance must be narrowed if economic welfare is to improve. Whether this is going to happen remains unclear.

In this chapter I assess Mexico's economic outlook for the medium and long terms. To do so, I examine the relationship between the economic reforms that were implemented before the 1994 crisis and those that have been made since then. I also discuss the steps that should be taken to improve Mexico's economic development strategy and the prospects for its timely implementation.

A Decade of Economic Transformation, 1984–1994

It is essential to keep in mind that economic transformation in Mexico has been an extraordinary effort, with few parallels in nonwar economies. The various actions that have been undertaken can be grouped in three main categories relating to (1) macroeconomic adjustment; (2) what is referred to as "structural change" or "microeconomic adjustment"; and (3) the amelioration of extreme poverty.

Macroeconomic adjustment centered on conservative fiscal budgets and prudent monetary performance. In the 1970s and 1980s several rules related to fiscal and monetary policy were broken. The public sector deficit was perceived by government authorities as a useful tool to promote highly desired economic growth. Government spending increased drastically in all sorts of public sector programs in order to satisfy the needs of a growing population (i.e., employment and provision of basic goods and services like food, health, and housing). Unfortunately, tax revenues could not match the increasing trend of larger government expenditures. The result was a growing public sector deficit that reached a peak of 17.4 percent of gross domestic product (GDP) in 1982—an aberration in today's worldwide tendency toward balanced budgets.

The main outcome of fiscal indiscipline was a significant increase in public sector debt that absorbed large amounts of domestic savings as well as credit from international markets. For example, in 1987 the stock of public sector debt reached 95.1 percent of GDP, with almost 58 percent owed to external creditors and 37 percent to Mexican lenders. This made Mexico's government a large borrower in comparison to the governments of more economically developed nations. Notwithstanding this, public debt growth (domestic and external) was insufficient to finance the gap between government spending and revenues. The government decided to print money to pay for part of its expenses, exacerbating liquidity in the economy, encouraging private spending, causing inflation, and generating a growing trade deficit that would eventually detonate the peso devaluation.

A first and important step in Mexico's economic transformation was to reduce this oversized public sector debt, which in turn could eliminate excessive liquidity in the economy. Fiscal and monetary equilibrium was a necessary condition for a stable economy. Structural reform tried to achieve a more efficient performance of the economic apparatus. It included such diverse actions as transferring ownership of literally hundreds of public sector firms to the private sector. Among them were very important ones like Telmex (the telephone company), commercial banks, mining enterprises, steel, sugar mills, and airlines. Similarly, different business areas were deregulated: obsolete permits to establish and operate private firms were eliminated; borrowing interest rates were liberalized, as opposed to previous practices in which the central bank determined them on all bank deposits and bonds; competition in freight transportation was introduced, and so on. A number of policies and actions were implemented to let markets work better on their own. Other components of structural change included external trade liberalization (lowering tariffs and eliminating nontariff barriers) and policies to facilitate foreign investment and allow competition from foreign firms.

Finally, reforms were made with the aim of improving the welfare of the lowest income groups. Economic reform was initiated under President Miguel de la Madrid Hurtado (1982–1988) and intensified during the administration of Carlos Salinas (1988–1994). These reforms aimed at changing the economic apparatus so as to achieve growth rates that would be high enough to provide sufficient employment within a noninflationary context. They included allowing firms greater freedom in determining prices and giving the private sector more responsibility for overall performance of the economy (see Table 2.1).

Table 2.1   Main Features of Economic Reform

Financial	Fiscal	External Sector	Privatization	Deregulation
• Liberalize credit and interest rates • Create wider variety of savings instruments • Finance public deficit by means of noninflationary resources • Privatize commercial banks • Allow foreign competition	• Balance public finance • Lower tax rates to individuals and businesses • Eliminate preferential tax bases in various sectors • Drastically reduce fiscal exemptions • Stimulate capital repatriations • Strengthen tax collection and fiscal management	• Lower taxes on trade • Eliminate nontariff barriers • Develop free trade agreements • Renegotiate external debt • Facilitate foreign investment	• Disincorporate nonstrategic industries in the following sectors: telephone, commercial banking, mining, agribusiness, steel, aviation, and food	• Liberalize freight transportation • Eliminate barriers to technological development • Eliminate obsolete permits to establish and operate businesses • Promote private participation in the provision of public services (electricity, highways, water, etc.)

The economic results of these reforms were impressive:

- GDP per capita grew 5.6 percent per year on average during the 1984–1994 period.
- Inflation was reduced from 80.8 percent in 1983 to 7.1 percent in 1994.
- A fiscal deficit equivalent to 13.6 percent of GDP in 1984 was nearly eliminated, falling to 0.3 percent of GDP a decade later.
- Trade liberalization was profound and widespread. In 1983 import tariffs averaged 100 percent, and all imports were subject to licenses. By 1994 tariffs averaged only 11 percent (the highest was 20 percent), and import permits were uncommon.
- In 1987, forced lending from foreign commercial banks was the only way to finance the current account deficit. In 1994, U.S.$19.2 billion flowed voluntarily to Mexico, U.S.$11.0 billion as direct foreign investment and U.S.$8.2 billion as portfolio investment.
- External accounts improved dramatically. Nonoil exports of U.S.$4.8 billion in 1982 were eleven times larger by 1994. Total imports of U.S.$11.3 billion in 1984 had risen to U.S.$79.3 billion by 1994.
- In 1983, real interest rates were negative, and financial savings shrank 17 percent in real terms. From 1988 to 1994 rates were positive and sufficiently attractive both to retain the savings of Mexican nationals and to attract financial investment from abroad.
- In 1982 there were 1,155 public sector firms, but at the end of 1994, only 213 remained (see Table 2.2 for more such figures).

The positive results of these reforms raised the expectation among Mexicans that the country was on the brink of becoming an advanced industrialized nation—an expectation that proved short-lived. Even with the evident improvement, economic growth was insufficient to generate needed employment of about 1.2 million jobs a year or make a dent in widespread underemployment (defined as laborers that work less than thirty-five hours per week), which in 1994 represented about 17 percent of the labor force. Insufficiently vigorous growth made it impossible to improve income distribution and began to raise doubts about the viability of exclusive reliance upon free markets and private ownership as a long-term economic development strategy.

What the previous figures do not reveal is that the benefits from

Table 2.2   Main Macroeconomic Indicators, 1984–1994

	1984	1994
GDP (billions of U.S.$)	175.5	366.7
Population (millions)	72.3	87.4
GDP per capita (U.S.$)	2,430	4,196
Inflation (%)	59.2	7.1
Fiscal (economic) balance (% of GDP)	–7.1	–0.3
Real borrowing interest rate (average 28-day Cetes)	0.2	6.6
Current account (billions of U.S.$)	4.0	–28.7
Trade account	2.3	–7.8
Imports	11.3	79.3
Exports	24.2	60.9
Oil	16.6	7.5
Nonoil	7.6	53.4
Capital account (billions of U.S.$)	–0.9	11.5
Direct foreign investment	0.4	8.0
Portfolio investment	0.0	8.2
Private sector borrowing (net)	–2.6	2.4
Public sector borrowing (net)	4.8	–1.6

Source: Grupo de Economistas y Asociados, based on information from the Instituto Nacional de Estadística, Geografía e Informática (INEGI) and Banco de México.

economic progress have been distributed unequally. President Salinas's economic strategy included the National Solidarity Program (PRONASOL), to ameliorate extreme poverty. The distinguishing features of the solidarity program were actions directed toward specific groups at the bottom of the social pyramid and requirements for recipients at the community level to contribute their labor to the development of the publicly funded works and programs.

The government has claimed favorable results from PRONASOL, but it has not produced reliable quantitative information to allow the program to be assessed concretely. A study by the Economic Commission for Latin America and the Mexican government indicates that the number of Mexicans living in absolute poverty (for whom income is insufficient to pay for food needs) decreased only slightly from 14.9 million in 1989 to 13.6 million in 1992. Consequently, criticism of PRONASOL has emerged along three main lines: its real impact on poverty alleviation has been negligible; it has been used as a device to help the Institutional Revolutionary Party (PRI) electorally; and, by creating a parallel mechanism to respond to social demands that bypasses municipal and state governments, it has contributed to the weakening of formal government structures.

The government never claimed that PRONASOL was intended to reduce income concentration; however, the link between poverty alleviation and a more equitable income distribution is a natural one to make. As seen in Table 2.3, the bottom line after ten years of economic transformation (including PRONASOL during the last five) is that income distribution in Mexico continues to be highly concentrated and is probably worse than it was a decade ago. The share of total income going to the four lowest-income deciles of the population decreased from 14.4 percent in 1984 to 12.7 percent in 1994, and the share of total income for families with intermediate incomes (deciles 5 to 7) decreased from 24.4 percent to 21.7 percent over the same period. The three deciles with the highest incomes increased their share of total income from 61.3 percent to 65.6 percent. Thus, the economic transformation of the past decade, even with the compensatory programs of PRONASOL, appears to have harmed the poor and middle classes, while leading to an improvement in the position of the wealthiest members of society.

Table 2.3   Mexico: Household Income Distribution

Percentile	1963	1975	1984	1994
0–10	1.3	0.4	1.9	1.6
11–20	2.2	1.5	3.1	2.7
21–30	3.1	2.5	4.2	3.7
31–40	3.0	3.7	5.2	4.7
41–50	4.9	5.0	6.5	5.7
51–60	6.1	6.5	8.0	7.1
61–70	8.0	8.5	9.9	8.9
71–80	11.8	11.5	12.3	11.4
81–90	17.0	16.9	16.6	16.0
91–100	41.9	43.6	32.4	38.2
Gini coefficient	0.5213	0.4942	0.6137	0.5683

Source: Grupo de Economistas y Asociados, based on information from the Encuesta Nacional de Ingreso–Gasto de los Hogares, Instituto Nacional de Estadística, Geografía e Informática (INEGI).

Despite a lack of systematic evidence-based research, it is widely agreed that PRONASOL was used to improve the political fortunes of the PRI, mainly by strengthening President Salinas's popularity. In this context, the hypothesis that PRONASOL's community-based structure was conceived as a potential substitute political party to replace the PRI gains plausibility. Finally, the claim that PRONASOL undermined the political power of formal structures of state and municipal government in favor of the presidency faces neither credible nor substantiated objection.

The issue of poverty alleviation is essential to analyzing Mexico's policy prospects because it involves a large segment of the population. Some recent estimates hold that the number of poor increased from 13.8 million in 1984 to 17.8 million in 1992. Resources to solve the poverty problem will most likely come from the government, which in turn could determine the path of economic policy. At the same time, a steadily deteriorating system for income distribution constitutes one of the main obstacles to improved economic welfare in Mexico, particularly in the context of radical free market policies devised to address the worst economic crisis in modern times, the 1994–1995 peso crisis.

Between 1984 and 1994, and particularly during the latter half of that period, the Mexican economy was substantially transformed. Macroeconomic policy regained the consistency necessary for successful economic stabilization, and structural reforms induced greater participation in the economy by private agents. This transformation was not trouble-free, as was made clear by a burst of economic disequilibrium in 1987 that worsened the public finances, inflation, lack of growth, and unemployment. However, by the end of the period economic expectations were high, and it seemed that the major obstacles to future economic prosperity were nonexistent or in the process of being eliminated.

Why this progress was interrupted will be debated for years to come. Was the economic strategy wrong? Did Mexico's leaders try to change too many policies at once? Were policymakers overconfident about the expected results of their actions? Answering these questions requires a thorough analysis of the way economic policy was conducted in the months prior to December 1994. The official explanations offered thus far, which attribute most of the blame to deteriorating political conditions, seem biased and shortsighted at best.

Causes and Effects of the 1994–1995 Economic Crisis

Much has been said in Mexico and abroad about the causes of the 1994–1995 economic crisis. It has been attributed by some to the "November mistake" (of not having devalued the currency in that month or even earlier) and by others to the "December mistake" (referring to the manner in which the devaluation itself was carried out). There were essentially three factors that brought about the crisis: the way monetary policy (liquidity, interest rate, and exchange rate policy) was implemented during 1994; the size of the current account deficit (which reflected a huge gap between imports and exports), as well as the means used to finance it; and the way in which trade liberalization took place (essentially a unilateral and indiscriminate import tariff reduction), especially during the early 1990s. In addition, the authorities made serious mistakes in the way they confronted and managed the economic emergency once it became apparent. As a result, the enthusiasm of domestic and foreign investors declined significantly, making the crisis even more difficult to handle.

Mexico's political situation also deteriorated in 1994. The guerrilla movement in Chiapas and the assassinations of presidential candidate Luis Donaldo Colosio and PRI secretary general Francisco Ruiz Massieu increased political uncertainty in a year of high political expectations. Congressional and presidential elections scheduled for 1994 were expected to constitute steps toward a more democratic Mexico. But the year's turmoil derailed this progress. Amid the combination of political unrest and inadequate macroeconomic trade, misguided exchange rate and financial policies turned an external financing problem into an unprecedented exchange rate and credibility crisis, one that was unforeseen by most observers and participants in the Mexican economy.

Even before 1994, several factors suggested weakness in some of Mexico's macroeconomic conditions, particularly in a growing excess of imports over exports of all types of goods and services, reflected as a current account deficit. This widening external imbalance was accompanied by an expansion of currency in circulation (liquidity) as well as credit from commercial banks to the private sector. Together these two factors promoted larger demand for goods and services, and since installed productive capacity was almost fully utilized, the growing demand had to be satisfied with imports, generating a larger current account deficit.

This deficit, as is always the case, had to be financed with a combination of external credit as well as foreign investment. New external credit and foreign investment accounted for the largest part of what is known as the capital account surplus of the balance of payments.

It appears now that economic policymakers wrongly perceived the effects of external capital flows over the current account deficit. The official view at the time was that the massive foreign credit and investment inflows (capital account surplus) allowed Mexicans to spend beyond their means, supporting a current account deficit of almost 7 percent of GDP in 1994. Consequently, if foreign capital inflows diminished for any reason, the current account deficit also would contract, thereby making exchange rate adjustment, as well as the need for any restraint on liquidity or domestic bank credit, unnecessary.

Events proved this expectation wrong. The interruption of foreign capital inflows during several months of 1994 meant a depletion of previously accumulated foreign exchange reserves with no sign of correction in the current account imbalance. Against this backdrop, the economic crisis was mishandled. An initial "managed" devaluation of about 15 percent on December 20, 1994, was insufficient relative to market expectations and lacked foreign financial support. The aftermath of these mistakes was an overshooting of the peso-dollar parity and an interest rate surge that in turn raised severe doubts about the effectiveness and endurance of the economic strategy. Mexican financial authorities tried to convince investors that macroeconomic policy was essentially correct and that only a minor adjustment program was required to regain economic stability. Evidence from before the crisis supported this contention in some respects; single-digit inflation (for the first time in two decades), a low fiscal deficit, positive expectations about economic growth, increasing real wages and employment, and a strengthened private sector were among the positive signs. The exceptions were growing disequilibrium in external accounts, increasing dependence on foreign capital inflows, and a stronger peso. A combination of these economic problems and errors in the way the crisis was managed provoked a crisis of credibility, an overreaction in the financial and foreign exchange markets, and eventually the severest economic adjustment program Mexico has implemented in modern times (see Figure 2.1).

Matters worsened when the Mexican authorities used monetary policy (money creation) to try to offset the effects of political unrest. The armed uprising in Chiapas and the assassination of Colosio led to an interruption in the inflow of foreign capital. Foreign reserves consequently diminished. The financial authorities implemented a "compensating monetary policy" that increased credit from the central bank to the rest of the economy (and as a consequence, more means of payment) at a rate higher than that consistent with economic stabilization. Beginning in the second quarter of 1994, the flow of credit into the economy—both internal credit from the Bank of Mexico to financial intermediaries and commercial and development bank credit to the private sector—increased considerably.

This "expansive" monetary policy was intended to avert a

Figure 2.1　From a Financing Problem to an Exchange Rate and Credibility Crisis

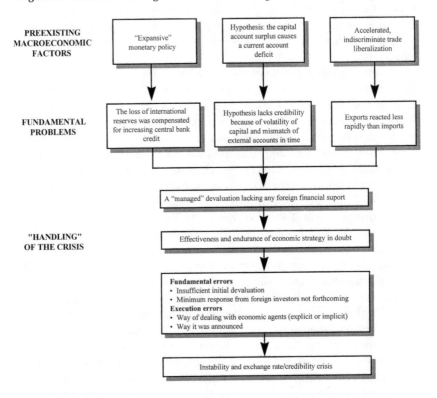

liquidity crisis that would translate into higher real interest rates and thus pose an obstacle to economic recovery in an election year. Rates did, in fact, fall as a result of this policy. It appears that the central bank's expectation at the time was that this expansion of domestic credit would be compensated for once the inflow of foreign resources resumed following the presidential elections in August. However, the foreign capital inflow did not pick up at the rate demanded by the economy, especially after Ruíz Massieu's assassination in September.

Over the short term, the expansion of credit prevented events in the political sphere from translating into negative expectations and constraining economic recovery. Ultimately, however, credit expansion had quite negative effects since it supported a private spending trend, increasing the demand for foreign exchange in a situation in which foreign exchange was becoming one of the scarcest resources for the Mexican economy.

Whether monetary expansion was deliberately implemented to

tilt presidential elections toward the PRI is unclear. The central bank autonomy was precisely designed to isolate monetary policy from political pressures. However, it is obvious that the way economic liquidity was conducted avoided an economic slowdown in an election year—and a crucial one for the PRI, since it included a presidential election.

Also, one of the biggest problems was that the monetary authorities seemed indifferent to the high proportion of short-term resources coming from abroad, which made them extremely volatile in nature. Equity shares and bonds constituted 56 percent of net foreign financial inflows to Mexico. Furthermore, although in 1991–1993 short-term dollar-denominated government instruments (*Tesobonos*) represented less than 2 percent of total federal government debt, by 1994 they amounted to 62 percent. The increased reliance on these instruments reflected the government's need to induce foreign investors to remain in the country.

Sweeping trade liberalization also had generated large deficits with regions other than North America and played a part in the growing current account deficit. The current account deficit has been mistakenly attributed by some to NAFTA. In 1994, however, over 70 percent of Mexico's trade deficit was concentrated in European Union and Asian countries, despite the fact that only 11 percent of Mexican exports were destined for such regions and 25 percent of total imports originated there.

Beginning in 1986, trade liberalization contributed to reducing inflation; however, the problem was and still is its nondiscriminatory nature. Although imports from the United States and Canada were partially compensated for by exports to those countries, there was no trade liberalization pact with Europe and Asia, which would have granted reciprocal access for Mexican products in those markets. By unilaterally reducing import barriers to European and Asian products, the trade deficit with those regions grew substantially.

The aforementioned monetary and trade inconsistencies created doubts about whether the government's economic program could be sustained in the short or long term and were expressed as soon as President Zedillo took office. Observers felt that the president's inaugural address and newly appointed economic team failed to emphasize sufficiently the need to solve the growing economic problem. Uncertainty was fanned further by the official economic program set forth in the 1995 General Economic Policy Criteria (CGPE).

The CGPE left numerous questions unanswered. For example, it was officially acknowledged that the current account deficit would increase from U.S.$28 billion in 1994 to more than U.S.$30 billion in 1995. Nothing was said, however, about the way in which such a deficit would be financed, which would require the private sector to obtain resources on the order of U.S.$20 billion in order to keep the level of international reserves constant during 1995. This amount would have required that Mexico receive over 50 percent of total foreign portfolio investment available to Latin America. It was clear that these projections were not viable, given that in 1994 Mexico had obtained only 18 percent of such resources. In any case, both international and domestic financial markets perceived these targets as unrealistic.

In this context the authorities wanted to implement a "managed" exchange rate adjustment without any other significant supporting measures. However, Mexican as well as international experiences have shown that an exchange rate devaluation, in order to succeed, must be complemented with various measures in the real sector (such as income or public and private expenditure controls) and in the financial sector (such as monetary and credit controls). Otherwise, the devaluation will only translate into inflationary pressures, which cancel out any positive effects. Thus, the 15 percent exchange rate devaluation of December 20 was both ineffectual and impossible to sustain.

Furthermore, the financial markets considered the exchange rate correction and the lack of any supporting measures insufficient to correct the current account imbalance. The suboptimal intervention by authorities in monetary markets made market skepticism even more pronounced. In the days immediately following the exchange rate "correction" of December 20, 1994, the Bank of Mexico carried out open market operations with government bonds at interest rates of over 30 percent, sending a clear signal to the markets that the 15 percent devaluation was insufficient. Financial instability followed, as well as an exchange rate and credibility crisis. In order to fulfill external commitments, the government created the Exchange Stabilization Fund (ESF). By means of agreements with foreign governments, financial authorities, and multilateral organizations, the Mexican government was able to muster U.S.$51 billion—approximately half of which was actually used. Also, a traditional structural adjustment program was signed with the International Monetary Fund (IMF).

However, the financial markets remained unstable, with both the exchange rate and interest rates higher than expected in early 1995. As a result, the government announced a series of economic measures with the main objectives of preventing inflation from canceling out the effects of devaluation, decreasing the current account deficit to a level congruent with the availability of external financing, stabilizing financial markets, decreasing exchange rate volatility, and allowing interest rates to decrease gradually. Additional short-term objectives resulted from the external financial support package, including agreements with the U.S. government and the IMF. These called for measures to facilitate the inflow of foreign capital, prevent capital flight, restore Mexico's net international reserves, decrease uncertainty in financial markets, and provide support to the financial system.

The main economic policy actions included the following:

- A restrictive monetary policy forced a monetary base contraction of 25 percent.
- A free-floating exchange rate system was introduced.
- Wage and salary controls were kept in place, with a 12 percent minimum wage increase beginning on April 1, 1995, in addition to the 7 percent increase agreed upon in January. Yet real wages still did not improve since expected inflation was at least double the combined nominal wage increase.
- Mechanisms were put in place in the financial sector to lower the cost of bank credit, including the introduction of instruments indexed to inflation (called UDIs) and the implementation of programs to restructure credits. In addition, mechanisms in support of commercial banks (as well as businesses) were established through subsidies or temporary capitalization.
- Substantial adjustments regarding fiscal matters were carried out by means of price and rate increases for goods and services supplied by the public sector. For example, gasoline and diesel fuel costs were increased by 48.5 percent annually; electricity and gas by 32.0 percent; and railroad, highway, and bridge tolls by 30.0 percent. The value-added tax was raised from 10 percent to 15 percent across the board, and a decrease in public spending was proposed (a 9.8 percent reduction in nonfinancial public spending in real terms, equivalent to 1.6 percent of GDP).

The economic adjustment program produced immediate positive results, although at a very high cost to Mexican producers and consumers. Figure 2.2 shows that most macroeconomic policy actions were directed toward decreasing domestic demand. Lower aggregate demand would in turn help to close the trade gap, replenish international reserves in order to stabilize the exchange rate, and keep inflation as low as possible.

Figure 2.2   Short-Term Macroeconomic Program

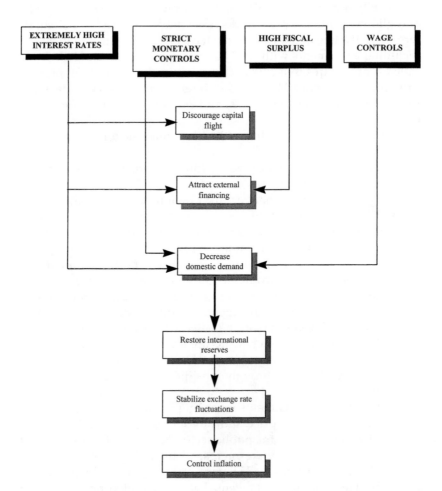

Two years after the onset of the crisis, the economic adjustment program showed rapid and striking progress toward stabilization (with inflation, interest rates, and the exchange rate essentially under control), as well as dramatic positive changes in the external accounts, greater stability in the foreign exchange market, and a reduction in interest rates. However, the costs of success have been extraordinarily high, and it is clear that they were underestimated by public officials.

The economic adjustment program achieved, at record speed, national self-sufficiency regarding foreign exchange. This implies that the amount of foreign exchange needed for imports, interest on the foreign debt, and other purposes is almost equivalent to the supply of foreign currency generated by total exports. This situation compares favorably with the U.S.$29 billion current account deficit registered in 1994. Self-sufficiency regarding foreign currency in trade transactions and services was complemented by income from moderate but voluntary foreign capital inflows. Both factors have removed any doubts about Mexican solvency, while at the same time lowering expectations regarding abrupt changes in the peso-dollar exchange rate. Within barely six months, the financial and exchange rate markets were stabilized.

This performance suggests that the economy was able to overcome rapidly the initial stage of the crisis characterized by financial uncertainty and generalized instability. However, a second stage, undoubtedly more complex, was marked by a profound contraction in economic activity and employment levels, wage deterioration, high real interest rates, decreasing levels of well-being, and the proliferation of social unrest.

Perhaps the most worrisome aspect regarding costs lies in the severity with which economic activity was affected as a result of the crisis. In 1995, the Mexican economy shrank 6.2 percent in real terms—the biggest decline since 1932. Economic activity contracted in all sectors: agricultural (2 percent), industrial (4.6 percent), and service (6.1 percent). The fall in gross national product (GDP) was significantly larger than the official estimate of –2 percent foreseen in the economic adjustment program.

The Mexican economy is no stranger to declines in economic activity. During the past six decades, GDP has decreased on five occasions (four of them between 1982 and 1995). However, the 1995 contraction tops all earlier declines. The situation is even more worrisome if one considers that the domestic market, which represents about 70 percent of GDP, decreased by 14 percent. This rate is more than double that observed in 1983 (the worst year before 1995) and contrasts unfavorably with the average annual increase of 2.5 percent observed between 1990 and 1994.

The challenge for the future is to foster sustained economic growth in both the export-oriented sector and the domestic market. In order to stimulate GDP growth, a reactivation of private consumption and investment, both of which decreased considerably in 1995 (by 6.9 percent and 29.1 percent, respectively), is essential. Together, these two components represent 78.5 percent of total economic activity, thus making their recovery essential to sustained GDP growth. As can be seen from Table 2.4, the extraordinary

Table 2.4   **Main Components of Real GDP Growth (percentage)**

	1994	1995	1996
GDP	3.5	−6.2	5.1
Consumption	3.5	−6.8	2.5
Private	3.7	−6.9	2.3
Public	2.5	−6.4	3.7
Investment	8.1	−29.1	17.7
Exports	7.3	36.4	18.7
Imports	12.9	−12.1	27.8

Source: Grupo de Economistas y Asociados, based on information from the Instituto Nacional de Estadística, Geografía e Informática (INEGI).

growth of exports was not sufficient to compensate for the contraction in the other components of GDP. Figures for 1996 show recovery of all of the aforementioned components. Except for exports, however, the real levels of domestic consumption and investment are well below their precrisis (1994) benchmarks. Domestic demand would not reach levels similar to those observed immediately prior to the crisis until late 1997.

Improvements in employment and sectoral activity were evident, however, and may continue in the medium term. Despite the fact that the increase in employment levels is still insufficient to provide work to all job-seekers in the labor market (approximately 1.2 million per year), the tendency toward massive layoffs and complete absence of job opportunities has been reversed. Real wages continue to deteriorate, however, albeit at a slower rate than in 1995.

Inflation is the area in which improvement has been most rapid. Compared with the various peso devaluations of the past, inflation has remained decoupled from the increase in the exchange rate, revealing an extraordinary economic policy effort to keep prices under control. In 1995, the inflation rate was less than half the rate of devaluation (52 percent versus 120 percent); by 1996 inflation had decreased significantly (to approximately 27.7 percent), and it may return to single-digit levels by the year 2000.

The control exerted over external accounts, in which the current account deficit amounts to only about 1 percent of GDP, is also noteworthy. As in the case of public finance, in which the fiscal deficit is less than 1 percent of GDP, that deficit is relatively easy to finance without hindering macroeconomic improvement.

In sum, Mexico is moving steadily toward macroeconomic stabilization. However, a similar degree of confidence regarding economic development over the next few years is not warranted.

Additional Reforms for
Medium-Term Economic Development

During the past few decades, Mexico has experimented with a wide variety of economic development strategies. As was mentioned before, in the late 1980s and early 1990s, price stability and economic liberalization set the tone for government policy. Free market mechanisms were chosen as the optimal way to transform the economy. Practically on its own, the government determined its economic and social priorities and concomitant structural reforms. Meanwhile, increases in the government's social expenditures (basically focused on health, housing, and food) were emphasized in an effort to better redistribute the benefits of economic growth.

Nonetheless, economic development has lagged in Mexico, partly because the government's attention has focused on economic stabilization and partly because there is no strategy for filling the voids left by market failure. Mexico is endowed with human, natural, and productive resources whose improved management would translate into greater well-being, but there has been no commitment to developing ways to use these resources adequately. The experience of various Asian countries has shown that the effective utilization of human resources is essential to stimulate rapid economic growth. In this section I address some of the limits to and gaps in Mexico's approach to economic development and suggest what might correct the situation.

The stabilization path is only one component of economic welfare. Judging from Mexico's own experience in previous decades, macroeconomic certainty is conducive to growth, but it cannot guarantee that the benefits of such growth will be distributed equitably among individuals, sectors, or regions. The previous discussion suggests that there has been a deterioration in personal income distribution; a downward trend in the proportion of national income accounted for by labor, from almost 35 percent in 1994 to 31 percent in 1995; and major difficulties in expanding the domestic market at a rate equal to export performance.

Another concern for economic development is the uneven distribution of regional economic activity. In 1995 about half of domestic production (48.6 percent) was concentrated in Mexico City and the state of Nuevo León, México, and Jalisco, and twenty-five out of thirty-two states accounted for less than 3 percent each of total domestic production. In part, this reflects growing polarization between export- and domestic market–oriented firms and between large and small to medium-sized businesses. This polarization was intensified by the economic crisis of 1994. It is also clear that the costs of economic adjustment and recovery capacity are distributed unequally, in large part because of various regions' production structures and export capacities. For example, in 1995 overall GDP diminished by 6.2 percent. Economic activity in thirteen states, however, contracted by more than that (in some cases by as much as 9 percent), and all but two of these states are located in the central and southern parts of the country. In the first half of 1996, GDP growth exceeded the national average of 3 percent in only ten of the thirty-two states.

This uneven recovery has generated substantial variations in employment. States in the north, particularly along the U.S. border, have reduced unemployment by 50 percent more than central states and by up to five times more than some southern states. It is no wonder that Mexico's most intense social conflicts are localized in the south.

These and other imbalances challenge the official principles underlying Mexico's approach to economic development. During President Zedillo's administration, as in those of Salinas and de la Madrid, medium-term economic planning has been embodied in a formal process. Various six-year economic plans have set forth goals for economic and social development. However, evidence suggests that since the 1980s, government efforts have focused mainly on reaching macroeconomic stability (sometimes with ephemeral results), while other development aspects have been relegated in practice to a lower priority.

It is difficult to disagree with the principles articulated in the National Development Plan (PND) for 1995–2000, published in May 1995. Some questions remain unanswered, namely, the same that have been posed since formal economic planning began in Mexico: How much of the plan will actually be carried out? Which economic policy instruments will be favored? Will the original strategy designed to reach the plan's goals be sustained? The actions described in the current PND do little to resolve these enduring questions.

The five main topics covered in the PND—sovereignty, the rule of law, democratic development, social development, and economic growth—respond to demands evident in Mexican society, some of them quite old and others resulting from the current state of affairs. By structuring the plan in this manner, the government has made an attempt to reduce the gap between societal aspirations and government intentions—a particularly important goal since such distance largely precipitated the economic crisis. As mentioned before, arrogance among most high public sector officials was widespread, and public criticism and social demands about economic policy were largely ignored.

The part of the PND dealing with economic growth addresses five issues: the promotion of domestic savings, economic and financial stabilization, efficient use of economic resources, economic-environmental policy, and sectoral policies. In most cases, ideas that have been applied for a number of years are repeated. Thus, fiscal discipline is emphasized as a necessary ingredient to generate stability and certainty; price stability is restated as the main goal of monetary policy; and the promotion of small and medium-sized businesses is reemphasized.

On previous occasions, six-year plans included a quantitative frame of reference for the main economic variables. Assessments after the fact have shown that results were consistently less favorable than the goals set forth in the plan. However, such quantitative benchmarks serve as a way of objectively assessing progress in meeting the plan. They also help economic actors react accordingly. The current PND aims at economic growth on the order of 5 percent, as well as an increase in domestic savings of 6 percent of GDP. Thus, it is estimated that external savings (mostly foreign credit and investment) should not be larger than 3 percent of GDP and that productive investment will have to be increased by 2 percent of GDP.

The PND also states that domestic savings are the basis for growth, and it points to the advisability of increasing them by an amount equivalent to the reduction experienced between 1980 and 1994 (from 22 percent to 16 percent of GDP). Total savings, particularly domestic, have clearly shrunk over a fifteen-year span relative to the size of the economy. Since 1987, the total savings to GDP ratio has remained practically stagnant, but its composition has changed drastically through increases in external savings and decreases in domestic savings. It is unquestionable that such a situation should be corrected, since a greater savings coefficient will eventually translate into greater consumption (or income), which justifies the fiscal and social security reforms stated in the PND. However, increasing domestic savings (and decreasing external savings) will not necessarily bring about increased growth.

For growth to happen, such savings would have to correspond to increased productive investment. The evidence over a fifteen-year span shows a clear deterioration in the gross fixed investment/GNP coefficient, from 27.2 percent in 1980 to 14.2 percent in 1995. Investment in machinery, equipment, and other fixed assets—not simply an increase in domestic savings—is required to bring about higher economic growth. In the 1995–2000 PND, actions oriented toward stimulating economic investment are minimized in contrast with actions oriented toward savings.

Productive investment could improve economic growth in at least two ways. First, it translates into a stronger demand for goods and services—particularly capital goods. Second, it increases productive capacity and, accordingly, the future supply of goods and services in the economy. There is a direct and positive relationship between investment and economic growth. According to Mexico's historical experience, whenever the share of investment in GDP falls significantly below 20 percent, economic growth drops sharply. For example, the ratio of investment to GDP grew from 1965 to 1982, surpassing the previously mentioned benchmark, and real economic growth over the period averaged more than 6 percent annually. When the share of investment dropped to 16.8 percent on average between 1983 and 1988, average GDP growth was almost nil (0.2 percent per year). In the first two years of President Zedillo's administration, the share of investment in GDP was at 16.4 percent. Higher savings could facilitate the financing of new investment, but unless particular actions are designed to mobilize resources from savings into investment, the desired effects on economic growth will be impaired.

Another objection to Mexico's approach to economic planning is that the guidelines contained within the PND are too general to be used to create actual programs and budgets. The PND is supposed to be supported by thirty-two sectoral programs that, according to the Planning Law, should define concrete government actions. However, three years into the Zedillo administration, some programs had not been completed, and those that were are too general to achieve any effective results.

Development requires a balance between free market mechanisms and selective government intervention. The experience of other countries suggests that economic development requires a combination of the following factors: increasing domestic savings in the economy; securing macroeconomic stability; mobilizing savings toward productive investment; increasing human capital; promoting the use of advanced technology; and spreading the benefits of economic growth among the population as much as possible.

The free market paradigm is an essential ingredient for some of these factors. It is difficult to imagine, for example, an effective increase in domestic savings in a system in which interest rates are determined by financial authorities—as was the case in Mexico for several years—in lieu of the supply and demand of financial resources. However, it also should be recognized that in some areas there are limits on the market's ability to provide the necessary requirements for development. Market efficiency may be hindered by inadequate regulations or by the absence of institutions that provide a framework in which the market can operate. Transition mechanisms aimed at creating new markets and strengthening fledgling ones are required. Under such conditions, there is space for government action to complement the operation of markets and accelerate economic development without having to expend a substantial amount of economic resources, as the following cases of financial sector reform and education suggest.

Financial Sector Reform

The financial sector provides a good illustration of the effects of government intervention in Mexico's recent development. For several decades the Mexican financial system was subject to exceedingly rigid regulations. In the early 1970s, among other restrictions, the services that each financial institution could offer were determined by the government; consequently, their realm of action in the markets was segmented. In addition, the government set the price of services and the yield of financial instruments. Financial regulation was gradually modernized, and by the end of the 1980s, government intervention in price and interest rate determination had been eliminated. As a result, financial intermediation grew quickly; for example, in 1995, bank deposits reached approximately 36 percent of GNP, a substantial increase from the 24 percent ratio observed ten years earlier.

Initially, growth in the size of markets may be necessary to support economic development. However, size alone does not ensure that markets will develop the necessary characteristics to contribute to economic well-being. The economic liberty enjoyed by financial markets in Mexico over the past ten years turned out to be insufficient to create, for example, a long-term credit market. Today, as a result of the economic crisis, the majority of financial deposits from domestic savers have maturity periods under one year. Even during the relatively stable 1991–1993 period, there were practically no deposit instruments with maturity dates longer than three years. This kind of short-term financial savings structure makes it difficult to finance the long-term maturities commonly required by economic development projects, such as infrastructure, construction, industrial plant equipment, and so on.

Within such a context, various government support mechanisms were necessary to complement the operation of financial markets. Perhaps the most important of these was the creation of an institutional framework to promote and channel domestic savings. The private pension system, which came into force in 1997, allows the creation of long-term financial instruments by guaranteeing periodic contributions by businesses and individuals for future retirement needs. Eventually such funds will serve to finance long-term maturity investments and also might contribute to the development of capital markets for the small and medium-sized business segment. Both factors will decrease the cost of capital in real terms, which in turn will open increased productive investment opportunities in the economy. Such a virtuous circle is expected to translate into more vigorous and stable economic growth, which will benefit employment and salaries. In the absence of determined government action to establish new pension fund institutions, financial markets by themselves, despite the freedom under which they have operated in recent years, would not have been likely to develop in this direction. At the least, the speed at which the free market would have reacted would have been substantially slower, as suggested by the experience of the precrisis years.

Education

The case of pension funds is promising for economic development; nevertheless, it constitutes only an isolated example of what could and should be done in other areas of the economy. Another case, this one dealing with the accumulation of human rather than financial capital, shows only limited progress. The support given to education in Mexico is insufficient to develop the necessary human resources to facilitate technology transfer in a range of productive sectors. A global indicator of this situation is the average schooling of the Mexican population, estimated at seven years. This level compares unfavorably with those for countries that have accumulated human capital successfully since World War II, in that it represents four years less than the average for countries in the Organization for Economic Cooperation and Development (OECD), most emerging Asian economies, and even others whose economic development level is similar to Mexico's.

The fastest way to increase labor productivity is to increase human capital. Effective investment in human capital yields high social benefits that are not necessarily internalized in their entirety by private employers of labor. Education is also an effective instrument for redistributing economic growth. A better-educated—and hence more productive—population would contribute to reversing the trend toward lower wages for labor, which in recent years have decreased as a percentage of GNP. (Currently, wages amount to 31 percent of GNP, down from 38 percent in the early 1980s.)

There are many problems that should be addressed within education policy, but one that has been neglected for years concerns the financing of higher education. About 85 percent of higher education is provided by public universities and 15 percent by private institutions. Demand for higher education has been growing by between 5 and 6 percent annually, and rising demand is expected to continue in the years to come. This means that in the coming fourteen years the service capacity of Mexico's higher education system will need to double. An institutional restructuring is required so that education quality does not deteriorate because of inadequate financing. Most of public higher education is financed through transfers from the federal government. The need to improve federal public finances during the past twenty years has meant lower real resources available for public universities in relation to their growing student body. This in turn has weakened the quality of education and sped the decay of educational facilities.

A viable solution to this problem proposed by some experts consists of substituting private resources for public funding and provision of educational services. Higher education finances could be privatized to varying degrees and in varying ways: by creating new universities that, although financially and operationally independent, involve some form of government participation; by channeling a higher proportion of those seeking higher education to existing or new private universities; by establishing an entrance quota to public universities; or by allowing low-income students to be educated in a private institution under a state-supported scholarship system.

It is clear that the quality of education must be improved. The amount of real resources per student dedicated to higher education needs to grow over time, ending the downward trend of recent years. Increasing the availability of resources also would be an effective means of improving the earnings of professors and researchers so that demands on faculty by students and administrators could be raised and gradual improvement in educational quality brought about.

Implementing any of the alternatives just mentioned is no simple task, although it offers an important social return. The initiative has to come from the federal government. Unfortunately, signals thus far lean more toward preserving the status quo than enacting real reform. Without a drastic institutional change in higher education financing, the quality of education cannot be expected to improve.

Agricultural Policy

Government initiative may be crucial for economic development in other areas as well. This is the case in the traditional agriculture and livestock sector, which has been subjected to important regulatory and institutional changes in recent years. This sector's contribution to GNP (6 percent) is relatively modest, compared with its productive potential. The changes made in the early 1990s to the old system of guaranteed prices for and subsidies of certain agricultural products, together with the ability to transfer the property of agricultural plots, which was previously forbidden, have not been sufficient to increase agricultural economic activity. In the 1993–1996 period, real growth in the agricultural and livestock sector averaged less than 1 percent per year—less than the rate observed in the five years prior to the aforementioned changes (1.7 percent per year).

Again, this indicates an appropriate space for government action on several fronts. It could help to create markets where there are none at present or where they are incipient; disseminate information about crops and other products that could substitute for the traditional production system; spread high-yield technology; and build infrastructure to facilitate production and marketing and access to agricultural financing under improved conditions. Without a combination of these factors, the gap will widen between modern, rich farmers and the majority of the rural population currently living within the traditional agricultural system.

Industrial Policy

As previously argued, the productive capacity of the Mexican economy, particularly for the domestic market, has been neglected in recent years. At the end of 1995, domestic demand represented 73 percent of total demand for goods and services, whereas production destined for the domestic market accounted for only 60 percent of the output of Mexican producers. GDP growth showed an average annual increase in real terms between 1990 and 1994 of 2.8 percent, compared to 1.6 percent in the 1980–1990 period. However, this indicator masks certain changes in the composition of supply and demand of goods and services that are important to economic development.

Early in the 1980s, total supply and demand in the economy grew at approximately the same pace. With the intensification of trade liberalization between 1988 and 1994, the domestic market began increasingly to fulfill its needs with goods from abroad instead of those produced at home. Mexican production destined for domestic demand increased slightly less than 2 percent per year, while production from abroad (imports) destined to fulfill domestic demand grew six times faster (12 percent). This gap between domestic demand and production destined for domestic consumption may widen even further in years to come. Evidently, the domestic production system and domestic demand are not strongly linked. Evidence suggests that although consumers may experience greater well-being as their demand capacity rises, those producers whose activity is related to domestic demand will increase their productive capacity only slowly, and growing consumer demand will be satisfied by imports rather than by domestic production.

As mentioned earlier, the relative weight of exports is still lower than the relative weight of domestic economic activity, meaning that even extremely dynamic export growth is not compensating for the sluggish domestic sector. In addition, the transformation of domestic productive capacity into export potential appears to require a fairly long transition period. This is confirmed by the fact that neither domestic demand nor domestic production geared toward such demand will recover the levels observed prior to the crisis until 1998, at the earliest.

In this context, there appears to be room for an industrial policy on the part of the Mexican government to facilitate a more efficient redistribution of productive resources in order to stimulate economic growth. In certain countries, governments and private businesses have clearly defined some of the industries in which technological support, the establishment of quality standards, and the positioning in certain productive chains justify giving them special treatment. In some cases, such special treatment has consisted of performance-related support in the form of credit or fiscal incentives. In such cases, well-defined rules and objective referees are necessary in order to measure performance. There is always the danger of selecting the wrong industries and even the possibility that incentives will be mismanaged, but if designed flexibly enough, such approaches can serve as effective tools for economic advancement.

In 1996, the Zedillo administration announced an industrial policy program based on three strategic goals: promoting exports; building a stronger domestic market (along with market-based import substitution); and reinforcing sectoral and regional economic integration. Unfortunately, policy actions appear to be inadequate relative to these goals. The government has resisted a more precise definition of the economic activities that could be promoted, even though evidence shows that in some cases a combination of government and private support could be beneficial for economic development.

One success story of combined government and private sector effort in the past is the automobile industry. Just before the 1994 economic crisis, Mexico's automobile industry produced more than half a million vehicles per year, generated annual sales of close to $15 billion, and directly involved almost 1,500 producers (including large assembly plants as well as small and medium-sized auto parts suppliers). The industry had come a long way since the early 1960s, when the government had decided to support automobile production in Mexico mainly by establishing import quotas. Subsequently, several measures were designed to promote vertical integration and increase domestic content in automobile production. At a later stage, some incentives were given to export promotion. Today, more than half of Mexico's automobile production is exported, which indicates the industry is cost-competitive by international standards.

A detailed after-the-fact appraisal of automobile regulation during the past three decades would certainly show many mistakes. Import restrictions probably were retained for too long, hurting the Mexican consumer through higher automobile prices; some regulations were ineffective for the purpose of vertical integration or acted as a bias against exports. But these mistakes were resolved through subsequent policy experiments, and the Mexican automobile industry at present could meet the most rigorous free market standards. This case suggests that society can accept that the way to economic success may be paved with mistakes, and that government action in some sphere is preferable to traveling unguided down a road into the unknown.

It should be clear that collaboration does not imply that the government will replace or crowd out private economic activity. In some instances, government intervention to remove obstacles for free market development is appropriate, as is exemplified by NAFTA and the financial sector reform described previously. However, in other cases, direct government provision of goods and services or stimulus to private sector activity is required when the latter's incentives are weak. Intervention could even be temporary, but a complete rejection beforehand of public sector involvement on purely ideological grounds is unjustified.

Since 1989 the Mexican government has insisted that if left

alone, free markets will create the best path for economic development. In general, the executive power has been strong enough to impose this view on Congress. This may change in the near future as a result of July 1997 midterm elections, which were very important for the democratic process in Mexico. They included congressional races (all of the Chamber of Deputies and a minority part of the Senate), six governorships representing almost one-fourth of Mexico's states, the mayoralty of Mexico City (previously, Mexico City's mayor was appointed by the president), and Mexico City's local assembly.

Elections were fair and transparent, and the electoral outcome implied a strong recomposition of power among political parties and also between the executive and legislative branches. In its almost seventy-year history, the PRI had an absolute majority of both houses of Congress. As a result, Congress generally supported presidential initiatives, including in the area of economic policy.

One of the most critical results of the July 1997 elections is that the PRI lost its absolute majority in the Chamber of Deputies, although it kept control of the Senate. This means that every economic policy initiative will now have to be negotiated, with the government no longer operating from a position of great strength. Since the government is unaccustomed to negotiating with the legislature from a minority position, the policy implications of this new situation remain unclear.

It is possible that economic policy will be more influenced by political parties and by members of Congress than in the past, which may present an opportunity to accommodate some of the suggestions and needs already described. There is great agreement among the main political parties (the PRI, the National Action Party, and the Party of the Democratic Revolution) on the need to create more equitable economic relationships, as well as a better distribution of the benefits of economic growth. All parties recognize that market forces are a useful tool to identify economic needs and allocate resources. However, politicians can more easily make exceptions for political reasons, compared to the ability of public sector technocrats to do so.

It is too early to assess if and how the 1997 electoral results will promote changes in Mexico's economic development policy. However, the new balance of advantages and responsibilities of the various players involved in the design and implementation of economic policy has created a promising medium-term outlook.

3

Political Dilemmas of Welfare Reform: Poverty and Inequality in Mexico

Guillermo Trejo and Claudio Jones

On the verge of economic and political modernization, Mexico's social fabric is showing critical symptoms of deterioration. Despite recent attempts to reorient Mexico's welfare system toward a pro-poor agenda, poverty and income inequality are on the rise. The current welfare system has proven unable to cope with these persistent problems and has been largely ineffective in addressing the social costs of economic stabilization and transformation.

To what extent will it be possible to confront Mexico's critical social problems within the framework of the new economic model—the program of stabilization and liberalization pursued by successive Mexican governments since 1982? What are the conditions under which market-oriented elites might introduce institutional reforms in the welfare system to make it more effective in dealing with poverty and income inequality? Will the process of democratization currently under way lead to the construction of a more effective and egalitarian social sector, or will only Chiapas-type rebellions provide the incentives for effective social reform?

The uprising of the Zapatista Army of National Liberation (EZLN) in Chiapas in 1994 has raised major concerns in Mexico and elsewhere in Latin America about the accumulated social costs of economic stabilization and liberalization. The fundamental question posed by the Chiapas rebellion highlights the long-term social consequences of the new economic model: Will the rural and urban poor find a place in the new Mexican economy? Will they come to benefit from the current set of economic policies, or will their living standards continue to plummet? According to the EZLN, the Mexican Indians have no place in today's economy; the North American Free Trade Agreement (NAFTA), called by the Zapatistas "a death certificate for the Indian peoples," was one of the factors that hastened their rebellion. The economic crisis triggered by the devaluation of the peso in December 1994 raised further questions about the social consequences of Mexico's current economic policies, convincing large segments of the urban poor and the middle class that welfare gains under the new economic model are indeed limited to a few.

The purpose of this chapter is to analyze the social policy of Mexican governments since the initiation of stabilization and liberalization in 1982. One of our main contentions is that successive market-oriented administrations of the ruling Institutional Revolutionary Party (PRI) have failed to articulate a comprehensive strategy to eliminate the causes of poverty and income inequality as well as to cope with the social costs of economic transformation. The negative short-term effect that economic adjustment and liberalization have had on poverty and income inequality is likely to persist in the long run unless the Mexican government commits itself to a comprehensive and active social policy aimed at securing basic human capabilities for all Mexican citizens. Evidence suggests that export-led growth alone is unlikely to reduce poverty and income inequality and, in the absence of an efficient and egalitarian welfare system, is likely to cause them to worsen.[1]

This chapter is divided into three sections. We begin by analyzing the evolution of poverty and income distribution in the 1982–1996 period. Although economic stabilization and liberalization have had both positive and negative social effects, poverty and income inequality have intensified across social classes and geographical regions since the initiation of the new economic model in 1982.[2] As a result, Mexicans today stand to profit unequally from export-led growth. Although some states in the north are likely to enjoy the benefits of NAFTA, large portions of the south, in the absence of new social and political opportunities, are left with three choices: continuous social deterioration, migration, or rebellion.

In the second section we analyze the social policy strategies followed by PRI administrations since 1982. We review the policies on education, health, social security, housing, poverty alleviation, and employment of the de la Madrid, Salinas, and Zedillo administrations. We argue that the history of welfare policy in Mexico is tightly intertwined with the history of presidentialism and corporatism. Social policy under the new economic model has been shaped largely by the presidential need to respond to immediate political and economic crises and by the veto power that PRI unions have retained over social sector reform in reward for their support of each successive stabilization program launched since the debt crisis. The poverty alleviation agenda, on the other hand, has been dominated by presidential politics—first by "hyperpresidentialism," which reached its highest stage during the Salinas administration, and later by the structural decline of traditional presidential authority under Zedillo. In the first case, a massive antipoverty program had little, if any, poverty reduction effect; in the second case, Zedillo transferred two-thirds of the poverty alleviation budget to state governments, leaving the country with no clear pro-poor agenda in the midst of the deepest economic crisis in contemporary Mexican history.

In the last section we analyze the political challenges posed by the decline of traditional presidential authority and the decentralization of political power in the context of rapid social deterioration and regional polarization. We argue that the gulf that has emerged between an increasingly rich and democratic north and a PRI-dominated, backward south raises the possibility of future rebellions and poses grave problems of coordination, governability, and national cohesion. We suggest that the federal government, checked by a truly pluralistic Congress, must play a key compensatory role in bridging this widening gulf between regions. Finally, we speculate on the conditions that may bring about comprehensive social policy reforms under the new economic model.

Income Inequality and Poverty in Mexico

Economic stabilization and liberalization in Mexico have had both positive and negative effects on poverty and income inequality. But as of 1995, the net social effect was negative.[3] Income inequality had become sharply polarized since 1984, and regional inequalities across states also had increased. Most studies conclude that poverty levels rose slightly in the 1982–1992 period.[4] And all social indicators have deteriorated in response to the December 1994 peso crisis and the fiscal crunch that followed.

As illustrated in Table 3.1, income distribution was negatively affected by the cycles of crisis, stabilization, and contraction that dominated the de la Madrid administration. After a marked decline in income inequality during the oil boom of the late 1970s, from 1984 to 1989, 90 percent of the Mexican population saw a decline in their share of national income in favor of the richest 10 percent. In 1984 the top decile of the population had 22.6 times the average income share of the bottom decile, while in 1989 this proportion had increased to a ratio of 32.9:1. During the Salinas administration, income distribution did not change significantly, partly as a result of an overvalued peso.[5] The total percentage change between 1984 and

Table 3.1   Income Distribution in Mexico, 1984–1992

| | % Income Shares | | | |
| | | | | % Change |
Deciles and Percentiles	1984	1989	1992	1984–1992
Bottom 5%	0.60	0.46	0.50	—
1st decile	1.60	1.29	1.30	−18.3
2nd decile	2.89	2.41	2.35	−18.8
3rd decile	3.78	3.30	3.20	−15.4
4th decile	4.72	4.22	4.16	−11.9
5th decile	5.91	5.26	5.14	−13.1
6th decile	7.32	6.56	6.42	−12.2
7th decile	9.18	8.26	8.33	−9.3
8th decile	11.94	10.67	10.94	−8.4
9th decile	16.52	15.51	16.10	−2.6
10th decile	36.13	42.50	42.06	+16.4
Top 5%	24.15	30.76	29.36	—
Gini coefficient	0.4740	0.5312	0.5313	—

Source: Humberto Pánuco-Laguette and Miguel Székely, "Income Distribution and Poverty in Mexico," in *The New Economic Model in Latin America and Its Impact on Income Distribution and Poverty,* Victor Bulmer-Thomas, ed. (New York: St. Martin's Press, 1996).

1992, however, shows a sharp decline in the income share of all deciles of the economic scale except for a substantial increase in that of the richest 10 percent. The economic recession of 1995 and the macroeconomic emergency program that followed in all likelihood had a sharp regressive effect on the structure of income distribution.

From the 1960s until 1981, extreme poverty declined and moderate poverty increased—although at decreasing rates. In contrast, in the 1980s the incidence of extreme and moderate poverty increased slightly. Regardless of the poverty measure used, extreme poverty increased during the de la Madrid administration. Primarily a rural phenomenon, extreme poverty affects large portions of the Indian population. In 1984 rural Mexico accounted for 64 percent of the country's extreme poverty, whereas in 1989 it accounted for 69.4 percent. Moderate poverty, however, remained constant or increased only slightly during these years. Between 1989 and 1992, extreme poverty grew modestly, and moderate poverty declined, although by a small margin.[6] As with income inequality, the 1995 crisis and the fiscal crunch that followed probably had a sharp negative impact on the incidence of poverty. Preliminary 1996 government figures estimated that 15 million Mexicans lived under extreme poverty (roughly 16 percent of the total population), and 30 million were moderately poor (about 33 percent of the total population).[7]

A study of the elasticity of poverty with respect to mean income changes between 1984 and 1992 reports that economic growth had no spillover effects on poverty reduction.[8] Poverty, however, is sensitive to income redistribution. The study concludes that under the new economic model, export-led growth is unlikely to have any poverty reduction effects. The reason is that the net benefits of export-led growth will be captured by the highest deciles and by those economic agents that are directly engaged in the outward-looking sectors of the economy. The rural poor, Indians, underskilled industrial workers, and the masses of informal sector workers will most likely be excluded from the benefits of export-led growth. Unless the federal and state governments devise effective redistributive and poverty alleviation programs, the study concludes, "the possibility of making export-led growth compatible with poverty alleviation seems to be rather limited at the moment."[9]

Regional inequalities have long been a feature of the Mexican economy. Whereas some states in the north today enjoy per capita income levels similar to those of South Korea or Taiwan, most southern states reach levels analogous only to those of Guatemala and Honduras. What is more important, as illustrated in Table 3.2, is that the gulf separating north from south is primarily a gulf in the level of basic human development. Whereas states like Baja California, Chihuahua, and Nuevo León are characterized by levels of human development (basic education, health, life expectancy, and political liberties) similar to those of the Organization for Economic Cooperation and Development (OECD) countries, states like Chiapas, Guerrero, and Oaxaca show human development scores similar to those of Central American countries.

Table 3.2   Human Development Index, Selected Mexican States and Selected Countries,[a] 1990

Nuevo León	0.889	United States	0.961
Baja California	0.870	Singapore	0.899
Chihuahua	0.827	Portugal	0.899
Guerrero	0.581	Guatemala	0.592
Chiapas	0.579	Honduras	0.563
Oaxaca	0.549	India	0.439

Sources: For Mexican states, Alberto Díaz Cayeros, *Desarrollo Económico e Inequidad Regional: Hacia un Nuevo Pacto Federal* (Mexico City: Porrúa/CIDAC, 1995); for selected countries, United Nations Development Programme, *Desarrollo Humano: Informe 1990* (Bogotá: Tercer Mundo Editores, 1990).

Note: a. Note that 1989 data were used for Mexican states, whereas data corresponding to 1990 were used for selected countries.

Although it is a structural feature of the Mexican economy, regional inequality has widened in recent years. Preliminary evidence suggests that economic and trade liberalization have had contrasting effects across regions: with relatively high levels of infrastructure and human capital, along with their proximity to the United States, most northern states have been able to benefit from the rapid and unilateral opening of the Mexican economy, whereas large portions of the rural and backward south have been affected negatively.[10] As illustrated in Figure 3.1, northern states experienced a reduction in poverty levels between 1984 and 1992, while southern states (particularly the southeast) saw a sharp increase in poverty.

Figure 3.1   Poverty Level by Region in Mexico, 1984–1992

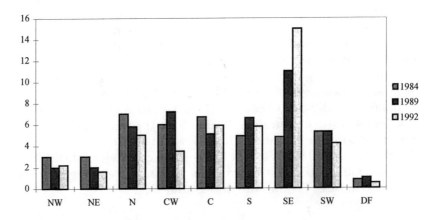

Note: Poverty levels are measured by the Foster-Greer-Thorbecke (FGT) Index; NW = northwest; NE = northeast; N = north; CW = center west; C = center; S = south; SE = southeast; SW = southwest; DF = Federal District.

The disparate effects of recent economic and trade liberalization raise new challenges for those concerned with Mexico's social landscape. In the next section we examine the social strategies followed by PRI governments since the initiation of the new economic model and the political incentives and constraints that have dominated Mexico's social agenda since the onset of the debt crisis.

The Politics of Welfare Under
Stabilization and Liberalization

The history of social welfare policy in Mexico is closely intertwined with the history of presidentialism and corporatism. The overwhelming power enjoyed by successive presidents, from the early years of Lázaro Cárdenas (1934–1940) through the administration of Carlos Salinas de Gortari (1988–1994), stemmed from their dual role as chiefs of the executive branch of government and de facto heads of the ruling party. Presidents directly controlled nominations of PRI candidates for all major elective offices and the appointment of party and sectoral leaders. Control over organized labor and peasants, however, was less direct; in these areas, presidents traditionally resorted to piecemeal social reformism as their crucial bargaining tool to elicit support for the regime and its economic policies. Mexico's welfare system thus evolved into a centralized hierarchy that connected the president with the different layers of the political system.

Established in the 1917 constitution and amended thereafter, welfare policy served as the material basis of consent for the sustainability of authoritarian rule for more than half a century. The Mexican welfare system, unlike those of the United States or Canada, developed on an occupational rather than universal basis and was founded primarily on social service provision rather than income transfers. The welfare system envisioned in the constitution was devised to satisfy labor's social rights, whereas peasant needs would be met with piecemeal land reforms and state-guaranteed prices of basic crops. In the 1930s, organized labor established a so-called historic alliance with the Mexican state under which labor sacrificed its autonomy and became a pillar of the PRI in exchange for the monopoly of labor representation (the "closed-shop" provision), a quota of gubernatorial and legislative seats, and the piecemeal satisfaction of the social rights contained in the constitution.[11] Centralized agencies were created to provide basic social services, primarily to labor constituencies. Unionized bureaucracies affiliated with the PRI emerged and rapidly developed the muscle to demand social rights similar to those enjoyed by labor. In the 1940s and 1950s, however, presidents retained the upper hand in the bargaining over social service provision. The influence of the expanding clientelistic networks of PRI unions was limited to the implementation of policies. By the late 1950s, the welfare system had become a privileged source of patronage that fed the growing network of clientelistic relations that converged around the presidency.

With the extensive economic expansion in the 1960s, the welfare system grew in size and scope; as a result, the network of clientelistic organizations that controlled the implementation of welfare provisions gained an unprecedented degree of power. The Confederation of Mexican Workers (CTM), the National Union of Educational Workers (SNTE), and various unions of bureaucrats affiliated with the Federation of State Workers (FSTSE) eventually colonized the state's administrative apparatus of education, health, and social security. As PRI unions expanded their control over the welfare agencies, the autonomy traditionally enjoyed by presidents in managing that system was curtailed.

These two trends—growing union control of social policy and shrinking presidential power over welfare policy—were not problematic as long as the country enjoyed the longest economic expansion of the twentieth century and authoritarian rule was accepted. However, when the legitimacy of the regime was shattered by the 1968 student massacre and the "Mexican miracle" came to an end, the constraints that the presidency faced in managing welfare policy autonomously became a fundamental problem for the sustainability of authoritarian rule. One problem was that the groups questioning the legitimacy of the regime—large segments of the middle class and the urban popular class—were not within the reach of the PRI's traditional sectors. A second problem was that traditional welfare policy did not extend to two potentially explosive groups: the underemployed population that had begun to thrive in Mexico's largest cities and the landless peasants that had remained in rural areas.

President Luis Echeverría Álvarez (1970–1976) made some half-hearted attempts to recover presidential control over welfare policy, but it was not until the administration of José López Portillo y Pacheco (1976–1982) that control over welfare policy was truly brought back to the president. With the creation of the Ministry of Budget and Planning (SPP), López Portillo parceled out an important share of welfare policy resources for poverty alleviation and regional development and placed these in the hands of the SPP. But the oil boom and the economic expansion of the late 1970s diminished the incentives for rationalizing welfare expenditure and the bureaucracy. López Portillo opted for a two-track strategy, funneling new resources through the traditional PRI-dominated social agencies while channeling petrodollars into poverty alleviation projects controlled directly by the presidency.

The onset of the debt crisis set the stage for Miguel de la Madrid Hurtado (1982–1988) and Salinas to pursue the rationalization of the welfare system during the harsh years of economic stabilization and liberalization. During the de la Madrid administration, social sector budgets were reduced dramatically. The government also eliminated a host of food subsidies that had mushroomed in the years of the oil boom. Following the original intentions of his predecessor, de la Madrid introduced a centralized planning system of regional socio-economic development under which the federal government would negotiate with each state government the size of the annual state development program. Also, in an attempt to decouple the welfare bureaucracies from PRI control, de la Madrid launched an ambitious program of administrative deconcentration in the education, health, and housing sectors. Finally, in response to growing political pressure from the urban popular movements that had blossomed after the 1985 earthquake in Mexico City, de la Madrid strengthened the urban development share of resources managed by the presidential cabinet and introduced constitutional amendments to provide all Mexicans (not just labor) with the universal right to health and housing.

Despite continual attempts by de la Madrid to undermine the control wielded by PRI unions over the welfare system, the unions managed to retain veto power over social sector reform. The acceptance of this veto power was the political cost to de la Madrid—and Salinas, six years later—for relying so heavily on PRI unions to control wage demands while suppressing the potential for generalized social unrest during the long years of economic stabilization and transformation. Discontent among labor constituencies was brought under partial control because PRI unions gained access to the perks and privileges that came with the colonization of the state-level delegations of the education, health, and housing sectors.

In contrast to de la Madrid, Salinas made social policy a cornerstone of his administration. Against the backdrop of economic stabilization and structural transformation, Salinas continued earlier presidential attempts to centralize welfare expenditure under the autonomous control of the presidency.[12] Drawing on the bureaucratic infrastructure and networks constructed over a decade at SPP, Salinas created the National Solidarity Program (PRONASOL), a massive demand-based antipoverty program that was controlled tightly by a core presidential elite. With PRONASOL, Salinas went beyond his predecessors' attempts to secure an autonomous branch of welfare resources in the hands of the presidency. In fact, after shaking the corporatist structure of the PRI by imprisoning the once almighty boss of the national petroleum union and forcing the resignation of the teachers' union boss, Salinas launched an unprecedented attempt to use welfare resources to organize a presidentially controlled base of political support parallel to the PRI. This was the highest stage of Mexican presidentialism, but PRI unions were able to arrest Salinas's attempt to detach the PRI from its corporatist roots.

With the prospect of Mexico joining the ranks of industrialized nations by the end of his administration, unusually high presidential approval rates, and an equally popular PRONASOL, Salinas faced no compelling incentive to push for the decorporatization of the PRI. Not only had the support of the PRI unions been a key ingredient in the continuous success of the economic stabilization program, but during the PRI's 14th General Assembly in 1990, the CTM had sent a clear signal that reforming the then sixty-year-old party would not be an easy task. With no strong incentives to reform the PRI and clear constraints on his ability to do so, Salinas avoided launching a definitive reorganization of the party. For the welfare system, this meant that, after the 1992 educational reform, the Salinas administration abstained from attempting any comprehensive institutional reform in other social areas, including health, social security, and housing.

Traditional presidential authority declined rapidly during the transfer of power from Salinas to Ernesto Zedillo Ponce de León in 1994, triggered by the assassination of the PRI's presidential candidate, Luis Donaldo Colosio, and the fragmentation of the PRI political class. Political change in Mexico since the 1994 crisis has been characterized by the breakdown of centralized hierarchies and the dispersion of political power across regions. The first and most important source of decentralization emanates from the PRI itself: after Colosio's assassination, the presidency ceased to function as the focal point for the political class. For the first time since the 1930s, the goals of many regional political actors no longer converged on the president. Political careers of PRI politicians in the post-Salinas era have come to depend more on regional elites—the state governors in particular—than on presidential will. The second source of decentralization comes from the growing cadres of opposition governors and municipal presidents that have emerged since the early 1980s, particularly from the right opposition in northern states and more recently from the left in Mexico City. Finally, further pressure for political decentralization comes from the demands for regional autonomy for indigenous peoples emanating from the Zapatista movement.

The fragmentation and dispersion of political power opened the door for the decentralization of the welfare system. Responding to mounting political pressures for welfare decentralization, and in an effort to dissociate his administration from the discredited Salinas government, in 1996 Zedillo agreed to transfer two-thirds of PRONASOL's resources to state and municipal governments. By transferring these funds, Zedillo relinquished the welfare branch of the budget that had served different administrations in launching presidentially controlled antipoverty programs since the 1970s. Unfortunately, putting poverty alleviation resources in the hands of PRI-dominated states is not likely to have dramatic poverty reduction effects. In the wake of the most severe economic crisis since 1929, and with poverty and income inequality on the rise, Mexico again finds itself with no effective strategy to cope with rapid social deterioration.

In over a decade of market-oriented reform, successive PRI administrations have failed to devise a comprehensive strategy to cope with the social costs of economic transformation and to address growing poverty and inequality. The approach of every administration since 1982 has been shaped to a significant degree by immediate political and economic crises affecting the presidency, and the implementation of reforms has been dominated by the political constraints of Mexican corporatism. Governments from de la Madrid to Zedillo have been unable to deliver a comprehensive strategy of social sector reform or devise appropriate unemployment and income safety nets, as the following sector-by-sector analysis illustrates.

Education[13]

Education was the first sector in which social reforms were attempted. The reform package, enacted in 1992, was triggered by a short-term political crisis: the leadership of the official teachers' union had shown itself to be incapable of controlling dissident mobilizations that, by 1991, threatened to reignite the popular mobilizations that had followed the 1988 electoral crisis. The launching of reforms demobilized dissident teachers, but once the political crisis came under control, the full implementation of reforms took a back seat.

Mexico's educational system developed around two pillars: the Ministry of Education (SEP), established in 1921, and the SNTE, created early in the 1940s to bring a host of local unions under a national umbrella organization within the PRI. SNTE was designed to resemble the highly centralized organization of SEP to facilitate policymaking and coordination. The union soon controlled decisionmaking positions in SEP and, eventually, the operation of the schools. Until the decentralization of the educational system in 1992, every aspect of educational decisionmaking—from the design and planning of educational services to their provision and evaluation—

was undertaken by SEP and SNTE. By the 1980s, the two had become, respectively, the largest federal bureaucracy in Mexico and the largest union in Latin America.

Reforms introduced in 1992 decentralized this system, giving state governments control over basic education and teachers' colleges. Despite this radical change, the educational system still faces serious problems: coverage varies widely across regions; average educational attainment remains very low, particularly in math and natural sciences; teachers are underskilled; schools are under the clientelistic control of the official teachers' union; and parental involvement in the educational process is discouraged by the General Law of Education and the teachers' union.

With educational expenditures at about 5 percent of gross domestic product (GDP) in 1994, the Mexican education system covers 68 percent of children of pre–primary school age, 92 percent of the primary school population, and 82 percent of the secondary school population. Yet one in every five primary schools fails to offer the six grades of primary school, and one in every five schools is attended by only a single teacher. The availability of schooling varies widely by region: although demand for primary education in Mexico City and the northern states of Baja California and Nuevo León is fully satisfied, educational needs in the rural and indigenous south and southeast are only partially met.

Average educational achievement is low. According to official data, in the 1990–1991 academic year, completion rates were around 50 percent, and according to standardized exams, only 16 percent of those who finished primary school met the minimal academic requirements of the primary school curriculum. Educational attainment also varies dramatically across regions. Mexico City, Baja California, and Nuevo León have better grades and higher completion rates than the national averages, but the rural states in the south and southeast measure well below national averages.

Poor educational attainment relates to several factors: undernourished students, poorly educated parents and teachers, and the authoritarian structure of Mexican schools. As for the students, according to private estimates, 30 percent of Mexican children under five years old are undernourished. States with the highest levels of undernutrition include the southern states of Chiapas, Guerrero, and Oaxaca. In the rural areas of these states, approximately 50 percent of the parents with children under five are illiterate. As for teachers' skills, standardized sample tests applied by the Ministry of Education to teachers' college graduates in 1989 revealed total average grades of 4.6 out of a possible 10. Underskilled and poorly paid teachers cannot help undernourished children and their poorly educated parents learn the basics of primary education.

Finally, problems with the student and teaching bodies are magnified by the authoritarian structure of Mexican schools. For decades, schools have been the locus of power for the national teachers' union, with SNTE controlling the appointment of inspectors, principals, and teachers. The evaluation and promotion of teachers depend on principals, and the fate of principals depends on inspectors. This clientelistic chain has a negative effect on classroom dynamics; in response to union demands, for example, primary school teachers spend approximately half the school day in administrative tasks.

Reforming the educational system has been a top priority of successive presidential administrations since the 1970s, when Echeverría first attempted to reassert presidential control over the welfare system. The decentralization of basic education has a long history of stop-and-go attempts that were systematically curtailed by the SNTE. In 1992, however, Salinas succeeded in launching reforms that decentralized basic education. Salinas's reform came in response mainly to SNTE's growing inability to control a dissident branch of the union that threatened to restart the post-1988 popular mobilization that already had been brought under control. The internal reform of SNTE under a new leadership facilitated the negotiation of broader educational reforms that included the following elements:

1. The federal government transferred the management of basic and teacher education to state governments.
2. SEP underwent a massive bureaucratic transformation, and its functions were limited to coordination and compensatory actions.
3. The primary education curriculum was redesigned.
4. A new system of teacher evaluation and training was proposed, along with mechanisms for merit-based promotion.
5. Councils of social participation at the national, state, and municipal levels were proposed to oversee the process of educational reform.

Under the Salinas administration, the first two objectives were met and the third was partially fulfilled, but the last two have not yet been realized.

In the long run, the outcome of reforms will depend on state-level dynamics, including the state's degree of electoral competitiveness; the governor's commitment to educational policy; and the relative bargaining power of the local branches of SNTE, local unions that have emerged in some states, and parents' associations. But in the short run, the success of reform depends critically on the federal government's capacity to implement its remaining components. The clientelistic control of Mexican schools will not change unless a new system of merit-based promotion is established, along with a transparent mechanism for teacher evaluation and training. Likewise, the ability of parents to contribute to the educational process will be limited insofar as parental participation is formally banned.

As the architect of the Salinas-era educational reform, Zedillo has made its full implementation his chief educational objective. A new system of teacher evaluation and training was established in September 1996, four years after reforms had been launched, but its meritocratic character will be limited since SNTE retains a substantial role in the evaluation process. The councils of social participation have not yet been created, and government and SNTE officials seem determined to keep the classroom door shut to parents.

The sluggish and partial implementation of the Salinas/Zedillo educational reform agenda highlights the limits of social reformism under recent administrations: although devised as a comprehensive program of institutional change, educational reform fell from the top of the presidential agenda once the immediate political crisis that had triggered reforms was brought under control.

Health Care and Social Security[14]

Reforming Mexico's health care and social security systems was not a priority until the December 1994 peso crisis. Reforms were introduced mainly to boost domestic savings and avert the financial collapse of the social security system, but again, a comprehensive reform of the health system remained low on the agenda.

Universal health care in Mexico was introduced as a constitutional right by the de la Madrid government in 1984. Although the constitution endows every citizen with health care rights, health care provisions in Mexico evolved historically as a response to the demands of the corporatist sectors of the PRI and hence are based on occupational rather than individual considerations. Health services are provided by the Ministry of Health (SS), the Mexican Social Security Institute (IMSS), the State Workers Social Security Institute (ISSSTE), and private institutions.

Mexico's health care system is tightly intertwined with social security. IMSS provides health services and social security to privately employed wage earners and is financed by workers, employers, and the government, whereas ISSSTE provides health care and social security to public servants and is financed by workers' and government contributions. Financed by government resources, SS provides health care services to informal sector workers and the unemployed. Since the 1970s, the federal government has subcontracted with IMSS for the provision of basic health care services to isolated rural and indigenous low-income communities.

Mexico's ostensibly "national" health care system has deeply rooted problems, including an unequal distribution of services among social classes, ethnic groups, and geographical regions; low quality of medical attention; administrative inefficiency, corruption, and lack of coordination; and questionable financial feasibility. Financed mainly by workers' contributions, coverage and the quality of health care provision vary according to income levels. In 1994, health expenditures amounted to about 4 percent of GDP and the national health system covered 94 percent of the population (IMSS and ISSSTE covered 59 percent and the Ministry of Health covered 35 percent). Like most health systems in Latin America, the Mexican system has developed a sharp urban bias in response to unionized urban constituencies. Coverage is higher in large and medium-sized cities, and the system emphasizes curative rather than preventive medicine (in 1991, 58 percent of the health care budget went to curative medicine, whereas preventive care received only 5 percent). As a result, although the urban metropolises in central and northern Mexico have infant mortality rates, life expectancy, and morbidity causes similar to those found in the United States, health indicators in the southern and southeastern states are similar to those in Guatemala and Honduras.

The national health care system, like other welfare institutions, evolved on a centralized basis. Formally, IMSS and ISSSTE are federal agencies that have regional delegations charged with the administration and provision of state-level health services. Although regional delegates are officially appointed by the directors general of IMSS and ISSSTE, in practice appointments are also made by the president, PRI governors, and by the IMSS and ISSSTE national unions. The regional delegations typically have operated along clientelistic lines, and inefficiency and corruption are common. IMSS and ISSSTE remain overtly centralized, with key financial and administrative decisions made in Mexico City, but the three health care institutions operate independently and service provision is seemingly uncoordinated. Lack of coordination has resulted in the misallocation of resources and overlap in the provision of services, even though coverage is not universal.

Mexico's social security system is managed by IMSS and ISSSTE. Both agencies provide social security to private wage earners and public servants based on employee and employer contributions. Employers contribute 76 percent to social security provided by IMSS, employees 20 percent, and the federal government 4 percent. The federal government contributes 64 percent to ISSSTE's social security, and employees provide the rest. Structurally intertwined with the health care system, social security reflects similar shortcomings, including insufficient coverage, an urban bias, administrative centralization, and financial bottlenecks.

According to official accounts, as of 1994 Mexico's social security system covered approximately 50 million individuals and their family members, or roughly 60 percent of the population. Large parts of the rural population and most informal workers, although potential beneficiaries of health care services, have no access to social security benefits. Contributions to IMSS from employers, wage earners, and the state serve to finance four different categories of insurance services: diseases and maternity; job risks; disabilities, retirement, laid-off senior employees, and death (DRLD); and nursery.

In the 1960s and 1970s, when Mexico's population remained relatively young, surpluses in the pension funds category (DRLD) financed chronic deficits in other insurance services and covered a host of administrative operations, the construction of hospitals, subsidized housing for IMSS workers, and recreational facilities. During the 1980s, the aging of the population along with shrinking welfare budgets and a long economic recession triggered an acute financial crisis at IMSS: although an unexpectedly high number of wage earners reached retirement age, increasing numbers of young job-seekers were not absorbed by a labor market in crisis and found refuge in the underground economy. Actuarial estimates made in 1993 suggested that by the end of the decade IMSS would not be able to meet its pension obligations.

Not until the December 1994 peso crisis did reform of health care and social security become a priority for the government. Under de la Madrid, some important but limited legal and administrative changes were introduced: health care became a universal constitutional right, a "national health system" was created (at least in name), and the administrative deconcentration of IMSS and ISSSTE was initiated.

Health care policy under Salinas concentrated on expanding

health services to the poor. As part of PRONASOL, the Salinas administration subcontracted IMSS to provide basic health care to low-income rural and indigenous communities across the country. According to official accounts, basic preventive health care provided by IMSS-Solidaridad and SS benefited 11 million people in six years. But no serious attempts were made to reform the system itself. Social security policy under Salinas was more aggressive, but reforms again were dominated by immediate financial constraints. The government introduced several measures to reduce the immediate financial strains on IMSS. Insurance funds were separated and placed under independent accounting systems so as to avoid interfund transfers. At the same time, the Retirement Savings System (SAR) was introduced to initiate the capitalization of a fund that would diminish the building pressure on the social security system while providing workers with a more coherent retirement scheme.

Reforms under Salinas and de la Madrid only scratched the surface of deeper structural problems in Mexico's health care and social security systems. More ambitious reforms were launched in the wake of the December 1994 economic crisis. In the stabilization program designed by the Zedillo administration, one of the key objectives was to buttress economic growth via a substantial increase in the domestic savings rate. By the same token, higher domestic savings would help revitalize a financial sector in crisis.

Reforms centered mainly on restructuring social security provided by IMSS. Health care provision remained for the most part untouched. The original reform bill sent to Congress in 1995 included the restructuring of social security funds and the privatization of pensions. Individual accounts for pension holders would be established and operated by private Retirement Fund Administrators (Afores). In an episode of legislative activism that reflects the decline of presidential authority and the emergence of an independent PRI agenda, PRI legislators were able to hijack the wholesale privatization of the pension fund. Responding mainly to union interests and local constituencies, PRI legislators shaped the bill to allow for the participation of IMSS as pension fund manager alongside privately constituted managers. In reforming social security, the Zedillo administration introduced a "voluntary" regime of social security that offers low-cost family health insurance for informal and self-employed workers.

Social security reform opened a window of opportunity for the concomitant reform of health care provision and administration. Without the possibility of interfund transfers, health care was left without its main source of finance. Nonetheless, the Zedillo reform left hospital operations largely untouched. Officials from the Zedillo administration and the IMSS doctors' and workers' unions failed to come to an agreement over institutional transformation of the IMSS medical centers. The Zedillo IMSS reform was thus a reform of social security but not of health care provision.

Zedillo did, however, introduce important changes in SS. Following the model of education decentralization, the federal government transferred the management of hospitals, budgets, and workers under control of SS to state governments. State governments are now expected to reach ten million Mexicans that are not covered by IMSS or ISSSTE, putting these governments under great financial strain. In meeting its constitutional obligation to finance IMSS health services, the federal government may also take resources away from the already underfunded SS medical centers to fund IMSS hospitals.

Health care and social security policy from de la Madrid to Zedillo suggests the limits of social reformism under market-oriented administrations led by the PRI. Reform remained in the background under de la Madrid; the reforms launched by Salinas and particularly Zedillo responded mainly to the need to boost domestic saving and bail out a financial system in crisis. Rather than addressing the deep-seated problems of the health care and social security systems with a comprehensive reform program, the Zedillo administration focused on the privatization of pension funds. Although some of the measures introduced, like the creation of an insurance package for low-income families, will bring tangible benefits to the poor, the larger reform of the health system is still pending.

Housing[15]

Reforms in the institutions that provide housing and housing credit have not been a top priority for recent administrations. The housing sector remains largely under the control of the PRI, particularly the CTM. Although some efforts have been made to extend housing opportunities to low-income families, a housing policy aimed at the urban and rural poor is yet to be formulated.

The Mexican constitution provides all Mexicans with the right to housing. Established only in the 1970s and 1980s, housing agencies emerged as a response to demands from organized labor and the bureaucracy. Housing demands of private wage earners and bureaucrats are met, respectively, by the Institute of the Workers Housing Fund (INFONAVIT) and FOVISSSTE (Housing Fund for State Workers). Financing for both agencies is provided by employer contributions amounting to 5 percent of employees' wages. The central bank administers a fund that combines public investment and private savings to finance housing projects for the middle class, and in 1981, the federal government established an additional fund for nonwage earners below a certain earnings threshold. Additional programs were introduced under PRONASOL in 1989, and housing credit and construction aid were provided to the urban poor.

Housing and housing provision credit face four problems: a large housing deficit; overcrowded housing; an urban and corporatist bias in house and credit provision; and lack of coordination among housing agencies. According to the 1990 census, 66 percent of Mexico's population live in overcrowded houses, and the housing deficit approximates 4.6 million units. Housing conditions are particularly poor in the shantytowns of urban metropolises and in rural and indigenous areas. Thirty percent of the population live in houses that do not satisfy minimum construction safety requirements; 34 percent of the nation's houses do not have sewage; 12 percent lack electricity; and 18 percent have no access to tap water. Differences among regions and social groups are significant: although most houses in Mexico City and the largest northern cities have sewage, electricity, and access to tap water, 20 percent of the houses in Chiapas have none of these services and 73 percent are overcrowded.

To the extent that housing policy has been shaped by political pressure from organized labor and urban popular movements, political criteria have prevailed in the allocation of houses and credit. INFONAVIT operations are controlled by CTM officials who have dominated the institution both in Mexico City and in the regional branches. Regional offices established in the 1980s and the appointment of delegates as in the health and education sectors have followed essentially political criteria set by the president and the PRI unions. As a result, INFONAVIT typically allocates credit and housing units primarily to unionized workers. Even when competitive allocative mechanisms (such as auctions) were introduced in the 1980s, the allocation of housing credit remained skewed toward satisfying PRI clienteles.

In response to pressure from urban popular movements in the capital cities of major states and in Mexico City, the de la Madrid government created the National Fund for Popular Housing (FONHAPO) to attend to the needs of popular sectors. Although the fund has been hijacked frequently by PRI-organized urban constituencies, FONHAPO also has served the needs of opposition popular movements. But the housing needs of the nonorganized poor remain unmet. For example, the fund does not reach rural or indigenous populations who receive practically no public housing assistance.

Housing policies during the de la Madrid and Salinas administrations responded to political challenges posed by popular urban movements that mushroomed in the largest urban areas, especially after the 1985 Mexico City earthquake and the 1988 electoral crisis. De la Madrid amended the constitution and introduced housing as a universal social right in 1985. Salinas's housing policy centered on expanding housing credit to low-income groups through PRONA-SOL and on reforming INFONAVIT's financial operations. PRONA-SOL housing programs were captured mostly by organized urban PRI groups and by independent urban social movements, seldom reaching the rural poor and indigenous populations. INFONAVIT's operations were limited to financial activities, and housing construction was abandoned. Management of workers' contributions was made more transparent by attaching them to the SAR fund.

Similar financial reforms were introduced at FONHAPO with the aim of making resource allocation more transparent and equitable. Although it is still too early to reach a final judgment on the operations of housing agencies, there is reason to believe that the allocation system still depends largely on clientelistic mechanisms: INFONAVIT's regional delegates continue to be political appointees of presidents, PRI governors, and unions, and the CTM retains a large stake in the administrative operation of the agency.

Changes in housing policy during the Zedillo administration were introduced as a by-product of the larger reform of the social security system. A new housing law was passed in the aftermath of the social security reform that introduced coordination mechanisms between INFONAVIT and IMSS in the SAR account. Also, a new mechanism was introduced to give laid-off workers the opportunity to refinance their debts and retain title to their homes.

The lack of any serious reform attempt in Mexico's housing institutions during more than a decade of market-oriented reforms suggests the priority given to economic stabilization over a housing policy aimed at the urban and particularly the rural poor. In exchange for its continuous support of economic stabilization, organized labor tied to the PRI has been able to secure housing benefits systematically since the 1970s. Housing facilities for the poor have come only as a response to popular urban mobilization. As in the areas of education, health, and social security, political crises and constraints have shaped the housing policy of governments more concerned with market liberalization than with comprehensive social reform.

Poverty Alleviation Programs

The history of poverty alleviation in Mexico is closely linked to the recent history of presidentialism. In their attempts to regain control over the welfare system, presidents from López Portillo to Salinas fought to keep a significant share of the welfare budget under direct presidential control. To this end, López Portillo and Salinas launched massive antipoverty programs; centralized and free of institutional checks, these programs became policy tools to generate political support for the presidency and the PRI and had little, if any, effect on poverty reduction. The decline of presidential authority beginning in 1994 put an end to these endeavors but ushered in a new era in which governors will be able to use poverty reduction resources at their own discretion, particularly in PRI-dominated states.

Poverty alleviation programs in Mexico were introduced in the 1970s by the Echeverría and López Portillo administrations. López Portillo built a dense web of generalized and targeted food subsidies benefiting the urban and rural poor, as well as broad segments of the middle class—whether they supported the PRI or not. De la Madrid dismantled most of the food programs created by his predecessor without offering an alternative pro-poor agenda. Thus, in the 1980s, economic stabilization and liberalization took place without an appropriate safety net in place.

Poverty alleviation programs were vigorously reintroduced by the Salinas administration, particularly through the presidentially-controlled PRONASOL. A demand-based antipoverty program aimed at the construction of social and physical infrastructure, PRONASOL became the backbone of Salinas's social policy and, as noted earlier, one of the key instruments of regime transformation. PRONASOL was initially implemented by state delegates of the now-defunct SPP. The PRONASOL bureaucracy was upgraded to cabinet-level status in 1992, and implementation remained in the hands of state-level delegates, now of the Ministry of Social Development (SEDESOL).

Although PRONASOL succeeded in some domains and provided some valuable policy lessons, its design and implementation had five fundamental problems. First, PRONASOL lacked a specific strategy for extreme poverty alleviation and failed to distinguish between moderate and extreme poverty. Second, the program served as a substitute for, rather than a complement to, social sector reform. Third, it did not include employment safety net or income maintenance programs. Fourth, PRONASOL was a presidential program free of checks by other institutions. And finally, the program's operations were determined by political and electoral—not welfare—criteria.

PRONASOL included three general program areas: welfare benefits, productive benefits, and regional development. With approximately 70 percent of PRONASOL's budget, welfare programs included projects related to physical and social infrastructure, such as the provision of housing, electrification, street paving, and water and sewage lines; school repair; and the construction of local health clinics. Direct transfers were limited to a scholarship program for needy children and to subsidized food staples. Productive benefit programs absorbed 15 percent of the budget and, since 1991, were aimed at financing micro-enterprises. The remaining 15 percent of the budget went to regional development in the form of soft credits to rural workers and to the creation of "popular" banks. Programs devised for indigenous communities were managed separately by the National Indigenous Institute (INI).

With its strong urban bias, PRONASOL addressed primarily the problems of the moderately poor. Housing, electrification, street paving, construction of water and sewage systems, school repair, and most targeted income transfers and subsidies were channeled to the cities. Benefits to the extreme poor were limited for several reasons. First, demand-based programs that require community organization do not reach the very poor simply because a community's capacity to organize tends to be inversely related to its poverty level. Second, since the extreme poor generally do not have access to the welfare system, housing and school programs almost never reach them. Third, although PRONASOL expanded basic health care coverage to rural communities, the program never fully addressed nutrition or health education. (International experience suggests that extreme poverty eradication requires the supply of targeted policy packages in these areas.)

PRONASOL replaced, rather than complemented, social sector reform efforts. With the exception of the IMSS-Solidaridad health clinics, the program remained uncoordinated with social sector ministries and other public agencies. PRONASOL followed a plebiscitary logic by which the president appealed directly to the poor, bypassing the bureaucratic apparatus of the social welfare system. Electoral victories in 1991, the popularity of PRONASOL, and unparalleled high presidential approval ratings reduced any incentive for Salinas to carry out broader social sector reform. After 1991, social policy under Salinas (except in the area of education) was shaped by successive accommodations with PRI union bosses, and more ambitious institutional reforms remained at the bottom of the presidential agenda.

During periods of economic transformation, a pro-poor strategy along the lines of PRONASOL may yield large short-term payoffs; however, to the extent that poverty alleviation programs substitute for, rather than complement, a broader, long-term approach, social reformism will be doomed to failure. The example of school repair programs drives the point home: the impact of refurbished schools depends ultimately on the quality of the education system. As long as the authoritarian nature of Mexican schools remains untouched, the net benefit of refurbished classrooms will be minimal.

As for the implementation of the program, PRONASOL was orchestrated and implemented under tight presidential control. Resource allocation was determined at the discretion of the presidential office. As a result, PRONASOL resources did not flow to areas most in need of poverty alleviation. Although in absolute terms resources were channeled mainly to Mexico's poorest states (Chiapas, Guerrero, and Oaxaca), on a per capita basis middle-income states (the capital cities in particular) were the largest beneficiaries of the program. Moreover, research based on the 1991 federal elections suggests that the allocation of PRONASOL funds was driven by political criteria[16]; after the 1991 PRI electoral victory, the implementation of PRONASOL varied across states according to the degree of electoral competitiveness and the capacity of the opposition for postelectoral mobilization.[17] In states where the PRI's monopoly remained unchallenged (for example, Chiapas, Oaxaca, Puebla, and Veracruz), Salinas's administration typically selected low-profile delegates to run PRONASOL and failed to organize grassroots committees that might challenge the political status quo. In these cases, PRONASOL resources tended to be captured by local party leaders and PRI brokers. In contrast, in states where the opposition was able to threaten the PRI monopoly in the ballot boxes or in the streets, the presidential elite opted for delegates with regional political potential and encouraged them to create grassroots organizations to cope with opposition threats. In sum, PRONASOL was more effective in the electorally competitive middle- and high-income states in the north than in the PRI-dominated, rural, indigenous, and backward states in the south.

Under Zedillo there have been dramatic changes in poverty alleviation policy in response to the 1994 economic crisis, the rapid decentralization of political power, and the growing discredit of Salinas's regime. Poverty alleviation under Zedillo has centered on extreme poverty. The much publicized PRONASOL gave way to the lower-profile Integral Program to Overcome Extreme Poverty. Zedillo's program concentrates on the provision of physical infrastructure; services to improve health, nutrition, and education; and employment safety nets to a targeted population. Sixty-five percent of the budget is allocated to physical infrastructure, 4.5 percent to individual services, and 30.5 percent to employment programs.[18] (The first two objectives are discussed here, whereas employment nets are addressed in the next section.)

Actions aimed at improving basic nutrition, health, and education are directly managed by the federal government. In 1997, the Zedillo administration launched a Food, Health, and Education Program (PROGRESA) to cover 400,000 families living in extreme poverty in eleven regions. The objective of the program is to eliminate traditional food subsidies (for milk and tortillas) and transform these resources (0.5 percent of GDP) into income transfers to targeted populations. PROGRESA aims at three population groups: pregnant women, children under five years old, and children of primary school age. Selected families with pregnant women and children under five will receive a monthly stipend (roughly U.S.$37) contingent on periodic visits to local health clinics where vaccinations, nutrition examinations, and health education will be provided. Income transfers are expected to be used to buy food. The monthly stipend to targeted families with children of primary school age will be provided only if the children remain in school. School breakfasts will be provided for children in the first and second grades, and income transfers are expected to cover the family's opportunity cost of keeping their children in school.[19]

Unlike PRONASOL, PROGRESA is a targeted program that aims at the root causes of extreme poverty: poor basic nutrition, health, and education. PROGRESA, however, is not trouble-free. First, the program targets households with incomes below the minimum wage; critics suggest, however, that the program has set this level incorrectly, underestimating the magnitude of extreme poverty.[20] To the extent that PROGRESA is one of the Zedillo administration's few pro-poor programs, underestimating extreme poverty may have devastating effects on those not covered by it. Second, it will be difficult for the program to reach the target population with the existing array of health clinics and schools, but provision of these services is no longer in federal government hands. Third, the implementation of PROGRESA involves only individuals. To the extent that Indians represent the largest segment of the extremely poor, the individualist emphasis of the program clashes with the community-based social and political organization of Mexico's Indians. Isolated villages tend to be highly cohesive, and relations between individual community members and the government are mediated by traditional Indian authorities. In bypassing indigenous authorities, PROGRESA diminishes the probability of reaching these elements of the targeted population. Finally, the financial feasibility of PROGRESA hinges on the elimination of food subsidies to the cities—a move that will create major political strife in large urban centers like Mexico City, Guadalajara, and Monterrey. But without these resources, the program will never be able to reach more than the 10 percent of the extremely poor that will benefit from income transfers in 1997.

Responding to the new political circumstances created by the decline of traditional presidential authority and the decentralization of political power, Zedillo introduced a law in 1996 transferring Mexico's entire physical infrastructure budget to state and local governments. By transferring two-thirds of the poverty alleviation budget to state and local authorities, he gave up key compensatory mechanisms available to the federal government since the 1970s. Resource allocation among states will be made according to a predetermined formula that takes into account state-level poverty indices. State governments, in turn, will allocate resources among municipal governments according to the same formula. Municipal authorities are expected to coordinate the provision of physical infrastructure jointly with newly created Municipal Councils of Development, composed of local community representatives. State and municipal governments are expected to address the physical infrastructure needs of the poor, but poverty alleviation will be subject to the discretion of individual governors, who are responsible for allocating resources (although municipal governments will manage the programs).[21] In the end, state-level poverty alleviation efforts will depend on the governor's agenda, on the state's degree of electoral competitiveness, and on civil society's capacity for mobilization.

In PRI-dominated states, particularly in the south and southeast, governors have moved aggressively to occupy the space left by the breakdown of presidential authority. PRI governors have become champions of federalism and state sovereignty and are preparing themselves to monopolize key political positions and resources in their states. The devolution of PRONASOL resources to local authorities provided them with strong incentives to gain control over

local groups of party activists and to safeguard a place for their lieu-
tenants in the state's city halls. Similarly, PRI governors have moved
aggressively to pack the Municipal Councils of Development with
PRI-allied grassroots leaders to ensure control over the disburse-
ment of resources. As the experience of PRONASOL attests, the
decentralization of poverty resources to states with autocratic structures will most likely result in the perpetuation of extreme poverty
and the fortification of the PRI's monopoly on power.

Poverty alleviation resources are more likely to reach the poor in
states and municipalities with high degrees of electoral competitiveness, particularly in the north. For example, in the northern city of
Tijuana, political uncertainty associated with electoral competition
forced the conservative National Action Party (PAN) mayor to
launch a poverty alleviation program that would compete with
PRONASOL. Experience in Tijuana reveals that the threat of losing
office pushes local authorities to respond to community demands;
hence, insofar as poor communities are well organized and have the
power to punish authorities in successive electoral rounds, poverty
alleviation programs are more likely to address the needs of the
poor.

Safety Nets: Employment and Income Maintenance

Employment safety nets and income maintenance measures have
been mostly absent from the social policy agenda of successive PRI,
market-oriented administrations. The new economic model was
implemented without any employment safety net strategy or specific programs to overcome economic contingencies. (The concept of
economic contingency, in fact, did not exist in the economic lexicon
until the 1994 peso crisis.) With economic and trade liberalization,
the Mexican economy has become more vulnerable to the volatility
of world markets. External shocks can have devastating effects in
rich and poor regions alike. For example, the inability of the federal
government to cushion the collapse of the international price for coffee in 1989 contributed to the outbreak of the Chiapas rebellion. But
economic contingencies also may have domestic origins, as evidenced by the traumatic experience of the December 1994 peso
devaluation.

During the Salinas administration, the only income maintenance
safety net available to protect the needy was PROCAMPO
(Agricultural Production Benefits Program). A direct subsidy program targeted toward 2.4 million small-scale agricultural producers,
PROCAMPO was introduced to cushion small farmers from the

social and economic costs of agricultural liberalization. Reauthorized by the Zedillo government, PROCAMPO is scheduled to last until 2008. As critics have pointed out, PROCAMPO is simply too small to cope with the magnitude of rural restructuring and lacks the resources necessary for the productive transformation of small farmers.[22] Also, like PRONASOL, its operation has followed electoral rather than primarily social and economic criteria.

To cope with the effects of the employment crisis triggered by the 1995 economic recession, the Zedillo administration responded by introducing an emergency employment program under the auspices of SEDESOL and expanding two existing employment programs. As part of the economic emergency measures, SEDESOL created 550,000 six-month jobs in the construction of physical infrastructure. The Training Scholarship Program for Unemployed Workers, a short-term training program that offered scholarships for up to six months, benefited 700,000 people. The Integral Quality and Modernization Program, a training scheme provided by private enterprises, benefited another 350,000.

Emergency employment programs devised by the Zedillo administration are clearly limited. Not only is the number of jobs insufficient to cope with present and future needs, but the jobs created are not linked properly to training programs and labor market requirements. SEDESOL jobs are linked to PRONASOL programs and provide no training. The scholarships provided by the Ministry of Labor, although tied to the labor market, fail to provide appropriate training and retraining. Training programs run by the ministries of labor and education, private firms, and unions lack coordination. The creation of public employment without appropriate training and retraining will have only a limited impact on Mexico's unemployment problem.

Most estimates suggest that export-led industries will not be able to create enough jobs to cope with the rate of growth of labor demand. Moreover, as suggested earlier, export-led industries are likely to create jobs that will benefit primarily the most skilled workers. Whatever the case, the informal economy cannot absorb an unemployment crisis of this magnitude, and migration to the United States—a costly option, as border controls tighten and measures like California's Proposition 187 (a proposal to refuse education, welfare, and nonemergency health care to illegal immigrants) gain popularity—will become less viable. These factors are likely to result in the dichotomization of the labor market, with a dynamic, export-led, high-wage sector on the one hand and a domestically oriented, depressed, low-wage sector on the other.

Political Consequences of Social Deterioration
and Prospects for Social Sector Reform

Poverty and income inequality have deepened since the crisis of 1982 and the initiation of the new economic model. Economic stabilization and liberalization have had both positive and negative social effects. Yet the net effect, even before the 1995 recession, has been negative. Despite prospects for renewed economic growth, poverty and income inequality are expected to rise in the coming years as the net gains from export-led growth benefit primarily the more dynamic and outward-oriented industries.

Regional inequalities also have widened since 1982. Northern states are rapidly entering a political-economic virtuous circle: higher levels of economic and human development are leading to democratization, which, in turn, opens greater opportunities for economic progress. In contrast, southern states remain dominated by the PRI and, in the absence of effective social and development policies, are likely to remain backward and autocratic. As a result of the failure of opposition parties to gain ground in the south, the rural poor will most likely remain without institutional channels to resolve their social and political grievances, at least in the near future.

Since the early 1980s, successive administrations have failed to cushion the social costs of economic transformation or devise a social policy strategy to eradicate poverty and reduce income and regional inequalities. Social sector reform has been dominated by the marriage of convenience between technocrats and corporatist leaders. Comprehensive reforms were successfully launched in the education sector but only partially executed. Similarly, the social security reform was driven by the need to raise the savings rate and avoid the collapse of the banking system, leaving the problems of the health care system unaddressed. In the eyes of successive market-oriented administrations of the PRI, the political costs of dismantling the complex web of clientelistic relations that dominate the welfare system thus far have outweighed the benefits of launching a comprehensive institutional reform of the social sector.

For the most part, welfare policy today is in the hands of state governments. Textbook analyses suggest that decentralization increases policy effectiveness to the extent that government officials and beneficiaries can monitor each other more closely, but the assumption that lies behind this claim is that states and provinces are homogeneous. In a deeply heterogeneous society in which differ-

ences cut across economic, political, and social structures, unintend-
ed consequences instead may prevail.

Decentralization of the welfare system in Mexico is taking place
in two very different settings. Most northern states are ethnically
homogeneous, economically advanced, and increasingly democratic,
whereas most southern states are ethnically diverse, economically
backward, and remain under PRI rule. Decentralization cum democratization in the north is likely to have positive welfare effects on the
standard of living of the poor; in the south, however, it is likely to
result in continuous PRI hegemony while increasing the potential
for social and political violence. To the extent that the structure of
power in PRI-dominated states reflects the national political conditions that gave rise to an inefficient and unequal welfare system in
the first place, it is reasonable to suppose that the problems that prevailed at the national level will be reproduced at the local level. A
weak federal government makes this outcome even more probable.

There are signs that the potential segmentation of the country
into a rich and democratic north and a poor, violent, and autocratic
south is already under way. The consequences of this process contributed to the political crisis that erupted in 1994; in fact, the rebellion of Mayan peasants in Chiapas is closely linked to the widening
regional inequalities of recent years and the decline of presidential
authority.

Originally a *rural* rebellion proclaiming peasant demands, the
Chiapas uprising evolved into an *Indian* rebellion heralding ethnic
autonomy. Political reasons played an important role in triggering
the Zapatista uprising, but the rural rebellion was stimulated by the
dramatic shift in rural policy initiated by de la Madrid and culminat-
ing in the reform of land tenure and the agricultural provisions of
NAFTA. Peasant expectations in Chiapas came down to one simple
idea: in "reforming of land tenure," the Salinas government had
given up on the *campesinos*.[23]

The Zapatistas "transformed" themselves from peasants into
Indians in response to new opportunities that arose from the decline
of presidential authority in 1995. As scholars of ethnic conflict suggest, movements for secession and autonomy emerge when ethnic
minorities perceive that disparities among regions and ethnic groups
are on the rise while the political center weakens.[24] The EZLN seized
this window of opportunity and introduced the discourse of ethnic
autonomy in the second round of the peace negotiations in 1995.

Chiapas provides important lessons for the future. The poor do
not rebel because they are poor, nor do they rebel as a result of

economic crises. Rather, rebellions seem to be the by-product of a combination of structural and subjective conditions. In a context of rising social and regional inequalities, in which the center weakens, external shocks that put the self-preservation of the poor at risk may provide radical political entrepreneurs with the elements necessary to persuade tightly organized communities to mobilize or rebel. The shock might be a sharp decline in the price of an important commodity (such as the collapse of the international price for coffee in 1989) or a dramatic shift in policy (such as the change in rural policy that culminated in NAFTA). Whether a radical policy shift puts the poor objectively at risk or not is irrelevant; in the end, what counts is their subjective beliefs and expectations.

By transferring the resources available for poverty alleviation from the federal government to the states, the Zedillo administration sent a clear message to the poor: from now on, the social policy of the federal government will be limited to a small targeted food program that in 1997 covered only 10 percent of those living in extreme poverty. For the rest of the poor, the only hope is to press their local authorities for social aid. In southern states, autocratic PRI governments have few incentives to respond. As suggested earlier, this reduces the options of the southern poor to three choices: continuous social deterioration, migration, or rebellion.

What are the conditions under which PRI elites and state governors might launch comprehensive programs to combat poverty and income inequality? Will only Chiapas-type rebellions provide the incentives for social reformism? Domestic and international economic constraints under the new economic model are indeed extraordinary. Sound fiscal and monetary policies are necessary conditions for the resumption of long-term growth. But a cardinal lesson that emerges from a decade of market-oriented reforms in Latin America and Eastern Europe is that economic reforms will not yield positive results if left to the "invisible hand." As recent neoclassical models of economic growth suggest, human capital is a key factor in explaining sustained growth.[25] To the extent that poverty represents the continuous depreciation of human capital, high poverty levels hinder the possibilities of long-term growth. Similarly, recent studies suggest that self-sustained growth is strongly associated with low levels of income inequality.[26]

Economic incentives for social policy reform notwithstanding, market-oriented PRI elites are constrained politically by their dependence on their party's corporatist structure to suppress wage demands and the potential for generalized social unrest while the new economic model is brought to completion. Most important, however, the means for social reformism lie today in the hands of state governments rather than with the federal government. As we have argued in this chapter, prospects for social reform leading to a more effective and egalitarian promotion of basic human capabilities depend largely on each state's political structure. Given the divergent patterns of political development that northern and southern states have followed since the early 1980s, we expect a sharper polarization of the country and, with it, problems of fiscal coordination, governability, and national cohesion.

Deepening poverty and the widening gulf among social classes and regions will be arrested only by an active federal government that is capable of mobilizing resources for compensatory and poverty alleviation purposes. As students of federalism have long observed, one of the key roles central governments are expected to play in systems with federal structures of government is to compensate for inequalities across regions.[27] The end of hyperpresidentialism has created an opportunity for opposition parties and civil society to introduce an agenda that would restore compensatory capacities to the center—in a manner different from that enjoyed by presidents from López Portillo to Salinas. As Congress becomes the new focal point in the Mexican political system, it could play an important role in overseeing the compensatory activities of the federal government.

Solving Mexico's persistent problems of poverty and income inequality requires an effective state and a strong civil society. An effective state means a state that is capable of formulating and implementing policies, that is open to society but not colonized by it, and that is accountable and responsive to its citizenry.[28] A strong civil society must be built by citizens who continually participate in public affairs and create networks of civic engagement in their local communities. Social policy cannot be imposed by technocratic fiat. The construction of an effective and egalitarian welfare system demands the continuous interaction of state and social actors at the federal and local levels. As Adam Przeworski and his colleagues suggest, market-oriented reforms may be sustainable over the long run only if they are opened to wider social and political participation through democratic institutions.[29]

Notes

We benefited greatly from comments made by participants in the discussion sessions in New York and Mexico City. We owe special thanks to Susan

Kaufman Purcell and to Eduardo Guerrero for their comments on earlier drafts of this chapter. Needless to say, we remain accountable for all interpretations and mistakes.

1. See Victor Bulmer-Thomas, ed., *The New Economic Model and Its Impact on Income Distribution and Poverty* (New York: St. Martin's Press, 1996), and Luiz Carlos Bresser Pereira, José María Maravall, and Adam Przeworski, *Economic Reforms in New Democracies: A Social Democratic Approach* (Cambridge: Cambridge University Press, 1993).

2. Humberto Pánuco-Laguette and Miguel Székely, "Income Distribution and Poverty in Mexico," in Victor Bulmer-Thomas, *The New Economic Model,* and Alberto Díaz Cayeros, *Desarrollo Económico e Inequidad Regional: Hacia un Nuevo Pacto Federal* (Mexico City: Porrúa/CIDAC, 1995).

3. This was the conclusion reached by Pánuco-Laguette and Székely in ibid.

4. For a summary of these studies see Guillermo Trejo and Claudio Jones, eds., *Contra la pobreza. Por una estrategia de política social* (Mexico City: Cal y Arena and CIDAC, 1993).

5. Carole Wise and Manuel Pastor, "State Policy, Income Distribution, and Neo-Liberal Reform in Mexico." *Journal of Latin American Studies* 29, no. 2 (1997): 419–456.

6. Pánuco-Laguette and Székely, "Income Distribution."

7. Secretaría de Desarrollo Social, "Aspectos Relevantes de la Política Social" (manuscript, 1996).

8. Pánuco-Laguette and Székely, "Income Distribution."

9. Ibid.

10. Díaz Cayeros, *Desarrollo Económico.*

11. Claudio Jones and Alain de Remes, "Corporativismo, sindicalismo y el reto laboral de México," in Arturo Fernández and Luis Rubio, eds., *México a la hora del cambio* (Mexico City: Cal y Arena, 1995), pp. 443–475.

12. John Bailey, "Centralism and Political Change in Mexico: The Case of National Solidarity," in Wayne Cornelius, et al., eds., *Transforming State-Society Relations in Mexico: The National Solidarity Strategy* (La Jolla, Calif.: Center for U.S.-Mexican Studies, 1994), pp. 97–119.

13. This section draws on CIDAC, *Educación para una economía competitiva. Hacia una estrategia de reforma* (Mexico City: Diana, 1992), and Gilberto Guevara Niebla, "México: Un país de reprobados," in *Nexos* 162 (June 1991).

14. This section is based on Clemente Ruiz Durán, et al., *Sistemas de Bienestar Social en Norteamérica: Análisis Comparado* (Mexico City: SEDESOL, 1994), Secretaría de Hacienda y Crédito Público, *Ley de Afores* (Mexico City: SHCP, 1996), and Julio Frenk, "Política Social," in *Este País* (October 1996).

15. This section draws on CIDAC, *Vivienda y estabilidad política: Reconcebir las políticas sociales* (Mexico City: Diana, 1990).

16. Juan Molinar and Jeffrey Weldon, "Electoral Determinants and Consequences of National Solidarity," in Wayne Cornelius, et al., *Transforming State-Society Relations,* pp. 123–141.

17. Robert R. Kaufman and Guillermo Trejo, "Regionalismo, Transformación del Régimen y PRONASOL: La política del Programa de Solidaridad en Cuatro Estados Mexicanos," in *Política y Gobierno* 3, no. 2 (September 1996).

18. Secretaría de Desarrollo Social, "Aspectos Relevantes."

19. Secretaría de Hacienda y Crédito Público, "Propuesta para la Reorientación de los Programas Alimentarios" (manuscript, 1996).

20. Rosa María Rubalcava, "Política Social," *Este País* (October 1996).

21. As different studies suggest, the resource allocation formula leaves great room for discretion in the hands of the governors. See Olivia Mogollón, "Pobreza y Distribución de Recursos Descentralizados del Fondo de Desarrollo Social Municipal" (paper presented at the Congreso Mexicano de Ciencia Política, Mexico City, September 1996).

22. Carole Wise and Manuel Pastor, "Mexico."

23. Neil Harvey, "Rebellion in Chiapas: Rural Reforms, Campesino Radicalism, and the Limits to Salinismo" (La Jolla, Calif.: Center for U.S.-Mexican Studies, Transformation of Rural Mexico Working Paper Series, no. 5, 1994).

24. David Laitin, "Transitions to Democracy and Territorial Integrity," in Adam Przeworski, et al., *Sustainable Democracy* (Cambridge: Cambridge University Press, 1995), pp. 19–33.

25. Robert Lucas, Jr., "On the Mechanics of Economic Development," *Journal of Monetary Economics* 22 (1988).

26. Tortsen Persson and G. Tabellini, "Is Inequality Harmful for Growth?" *American Economic Review* 84, no. 3 (1994).

27. For a detailed discussion of this issue, see Díaz Cayeros, *Desarrollo Económico.*

28. Guillermo O'Donnell, "Poverty and Inequality in Latin America: Some Political Reflections" (Notre Dame, Ind.: The Helen Kellogg Institute, Working Paper Series, no. 25, July 1996).

29. Luiz Carlos Bresser Pereira, José María Maravall, and Adam Przeworski, *Economic Reforms.*

4

The New
U.S.-Mexico Relationship

Susan Kaufman Purcell

Mexico and the United States differ in two important ways that have strongly affected their bilateral relationship. The most obvious concerns the difference between their levels of development. Mexico, one of the most important developing countries, shares a 2,000-mile border with the United States, the most economically advanced country in the world. The two countries also have different political systems. For nearly seventy years, Mexico has been a relatively stable authoritarian regime ruled by a dominant political party, the Institutional Revolutionary Party (PRI). Its neighbor to the north, in contrast, has been one of the world's leading democracies.

During the 1990s, two events occurred that hold the promise of reducing the contrasts between these two countries. The creation of a North American free trade area on January 1, 1994, that included Mexico, Canada, and the United States aimed at increasing the level of prosperity of all three partners. For Mexico in particular it offered the possibility of moving from Third World to First World status. And on July 6, 1997, Mexico's midterm elections undermined the PRI's control of the country's Congress and brought a left-of-center opposition mayor to power in the Federal District. Both election results transformed Mexico overnight from an authoritarian regime into a pluralistic, although still weakly institutionalized, democracy.

The impact that the North American Free Trade Agreement (NAFTA) and Mexico's transition to democracy will have on U.S.-Mexican relations remains unclear. They will certainly make bilateral relations more complicated. Because of the accelerating economic integration between Mexico and the United States, the line between domestic and foreign policies has become increasingly blurred on both sides of the border. As a result, the number and variety of domestic groups involved in what were traditional foreign policy issues will continue to grow in both countries. Furthermore, the democratization of the Mexican political system means that the Mexican Congress will now assume an important role in U.S.-Mexican relations. As a result, Mexico, like the United States, will now speak with more than one main voice on bilateral issues.

The fact that bilateral relations will become more complicated does not, however, necessarily mean that the interests of the United States and Mexico must or will diverge. The history of U.S.-Mexican relations includes periods when the two countries worked well together and appeared to share many interests and others when they seemed like two ships passing in the night. The end of the Cold War seemed to mark the beginning of one of the more cooperative and constructive phases of the bilateral relationship. The addition of opposition-party voices to the policy debates within Mexico could indeed signal a return to conflict, or it could mark the beginning of a more honest and open relationship that leads to greater mutual understanding and a willingness to work constructively to manage or solve bilateral problems.

From Diverging to Converging Interests

The fact that Mexico has been governed by a single, dominant political party since 1929 has not meant that its foreign or domestic policy has essentially followed the same line over time. Instead, Mexico's policies have reflected the differing values and interests of its specific presidents, as well as the changing opportunities and constraints facing them both internally and abroad. As a result, the conventional wisdom that it has been easier for the United States to deal with an authoritarian, rather than democratic, Mexico is not correct. At times the authoritarian nature of the Mexican political system has produced rather abrupt changes in Mexico's policies, often with highly negative implications for U.S. interests.

Stated differently, authoritarianism in Mexico produced domestic political stability, particularly when compared with the rest of Latin America. However, it also enabled the country's leaders to suddenly change Mexico's foreign policy in ways that were harmful to the United States and that might not have been as feasible had its leaders been obliged to obtain the consent of the governed. The United States, of course, also did not pursue consistent policies toward Mexico during this same period. As a democratic country with an independent Congress, however, there was never the same expectation that it would do so.

The one constant in the U.S.-Mexico relationship is that it has been "special" because of the 2,000-mile shared border between the two countries. Unfortunately, the term has often been understood differently on each side of the border. As a global superpower throughout most of the twentieth century, the United States wanted Mexico to be a stable, predictable, and friendly ally in preventing powers hostile to the United States from expanding their influence in Washington's "backyard." Mexico, in contrast, believed that a special relationship with the United States meant that Washington would provide it with resources and other privileges for it to become a modern industrial nation.

Each country unfortunately ended up disappointing the other. Mexico came to look upon its shared border with the United States more as a threat than as an opportunity. In part, this was a legacy from the nineteenth century, when the United States had acquired half of Mexico's territory. During the twentieth century, the United States eschewed outright military intervention in favor of less tangible forms of interference. The growing importance of U.S. multinational corporations in Mexico's economy, combined with the influence of new technologies such as television, led Mexican politicians and intellectuals in particular to focus instead on threats to Mexican sovereignty, culture, and identity emanating from the north.

These concerns became more explicit during the 1970s with the creation of the so-called Third World voting bloc in the United Nations and with efforts by Mexican president Luis Echeverría Álvarez (1970–1976) to lead it. In the process, anti-Americanism in Mexico increased. The mutual gains to be had from a more cooperative relationship with Washington were downplayed or ignored. Instead, Mexico's "victimization" at the hands of "the colossus of the north" was emphasized.

The discovery of vast oil reserves in Mexico in the mid-1970s facilitated Mexico's efforts at Third World leadership. Echeverría's successor, José López Portillo y Pacheco (1976–1982), chose to further remove Mexico from Washington's shadow by pursuing an anti-American, pro–Third World foreign and domestic policy. At home, this took the form of increasing Mexico's control of, and restrictions on, the entry and behavior of foreign capital, most of which came from the United States.

The 1970s did not mark the first time that modern Mexico had tried to pursue a very different economic path from that which Washington would have preferred. During the 1930s, under the leadership of President Lázaro Cárdenas (1934–1940), Mexico nationalized its petroleum industry and railroads and veered in a decidedly socialist direction in both its politics and its economic policy. Nevertheless, the impending world war encouraged the United States to smooth over its differences with the Mexican government in the interests of having a stable and friendly government on its southern border. With the end of the war, Mexico's new president, Miguel Alemán Valdés (1946–1952), abruptly changed his country's course and used foreign investment to launch Mexico on the road to industrialization.

Washington's reaction to the Echeverría and López Portillo policies was somewhat reminiscent of its behavior during the Cárdenas years, but for different reasons. Initially, the United States did not react strongly to Mexico's attempts in the 1970s to pursue foreign and domestic policies at odds with what Washington might have preferred. These were the years of U.S.-Soviet détente, which resulted in a U.S. policy of so-called benign neglect toward Latin America, including Mexico. Only in 1979, with the Sandinista victory in Nicaragua, did Washington's preoccupation with security issues concerning Mexico resurface. The very different policies that the United States and Mexico pursued toward Nicaragua in particular and Central America in general into the mid-1980s greatly increased bilateral conflict. Mexico strongly opposed U.S. support for the contras, favoring instead a negotiated settlement in Nicaragua and elsewhere in Central America. Mexico also challenged Washington's belief that the Sandinista regime constituted a security threat to Mexico and the rest of the hemisphere. The Reagan administration regarded the Mexican government's policies as unhelpful and naive.

Two developments in the 1980s, however, caused both Mexico and the United States to play down their disagreements and focus instead on their converging interests. The first was the debt crisis of 1982. The second was the collapse of the Soviet Union and the end of the Cold War.

The debt crisis, which was triggered by Mexico's inability to repay its dollar-denominated loans at a time of rising global interest rates, led Mexican as well as U.S. government officials to fear a possible collapse of Mexico's economy and its political system. The fact that Central America was in revolutionary ferment added to these concerns. The Reagan administration therefore gave top priority to stabilizing the Mexican economy via credits, swap lines, and other types of assistance. At the same time Mexico's new vulnerability, combined with the high economic cost of pursing an active foreign policy, caused the administration of Miguel de la Madrid Hurtado (1982–1988) to turn inward, thereby substantially reducing its involvement in the Central American conflict. The change removed a major irritant to U.S.-Mexican relations at a time when Mexico needed Washington's help and the Reagan administration needed congressional support in order to provide it.

The debt crisis also marked the beginning of the end of Mexico's industrialization policy known as import-substitution industrialization (ISI), which Washington as well as many Mexicans had come to regard as an inefficient and costly economic development strategy. The United States especially disliked Mexico's hostile attitude toward foreign investment and multinational corporations, as well as the emphasis on a large state role in the economy and the attitude of distrust toward the private sector. Nor did U.S. exporters like the high tariffs inherent in the ISI model.

The de la Madrid administration's inability to borrow money after the debt crisis in order to sustain the ISI strategy obliged it to begin opening the Mexican economy to foreign investment and imports. The latter offered competition to Mexican producers and required them to become more efficient, thereby increasing Mexico's ability to export in competitive global markets in order to earn hard currency. Opening the economy also helped reduce inflation. President de la Madrid also brought Mexico into the General Agreement on Tariffs and Trade (GATT), which provided concrete evidence of Mexico's decision to become more actively integrated into the global economy. And he began closing or privatizing inefficient state enterprises that had become a financial drain on the country.

As a result of Mexico's new, more open development strategy, the U.S. and Mexican economic growth strategies became more congruent. This was good not only for the bilateral relationship; it also brought to power new economic and political elites who favored and needed closer economic cooperation with the United States. Many of them had earned advanced degrees from major U.S. universities. Their knowledge of and experience with the United States made them more comfortable with their northern neighbor than had been true of their predecessors.

The really big improvement in U.S.-Mexican relations, however, occurred after the collapse of the Soviet Union and the end of the Cold War in 1989. These events coincided with the advent of new administrations in both the United States and Mexico. In the United States, Ronald Reagan, a hard-line anticommunist Cold Warrior, was succeeded by George Bush, a moderate Republican. He moved quickly to change Washington's policy toward Central America, most notably by ending U.S. aid to the contras. His decision was the result of his less ideological stance and, in addition, reflected the lack of support for the Reagan policy by the Democratic Congress. President Bush also pressed for elections and a diplomatic settlement of the civil war in Nicaragua. These moves removed the key irritants to good relations with Mexico. They were also touted in Mexico, rightly or wrongly, as a vindication of policies advocated by previous Mexican administrations.

The Bush administration was also characterized by an unusually large number of key officials who had lived and worked in Texas, starting with the president himself. They instinctively understood Mexico's importance to the United States in ways that Washington "insiders" often have not and were comfortable working with Mexican officials.

Carlos Salinas de Gortari (1988–1994), the new Mexican president, was part of a younger generation of political elites. Even more than his predecessor, President Salinas recruited to his administration internationally oriented young economists who had studied in the United States and who strongly favored deepening Mexico's integration into the world economy. The president originally intended to do this by moving Mexico closer to Europe and Asia, rather than to the United States. Therefore, he was not initially a supporter of a free trade agreement with Washington, an idea first proposed by Ronald Reagan in the early 1980s. He quickly came to realize, however, that Europe was more concerned with the emerging single European market and with the newly independent Eastern European countries than with Mexico. At the same time, Japan was preoccupied with forging closer links with Southeast Asia. President Salinas therefore changed his mind and proposed a free trade agreement between Mexico and the United States. He then unilaterally continued to lower tariffs and other barriers to free trade, accelerated the privatization of state enterprises, and implemented an anti-inflation program to make Mexico a more attractive trade partner for the United States.

President Salinas's economic policies did not reflect the thinking of either the Mexican Congress or the Mexican people at the time of their implementation. Instead, the president's political strategy involved implementing the reforms that he believed were needed to revive the Mexican economy. The resumption of economic growth would then help create the political support to sustain the new reform agenda. Whereas only a decade or so earlier Mexico's authoritarian political system had allowed President Echeverría to move abruptly toward a statist, protectionist policy, the same system, which gave its presidents great power, now allowed another president to move the Mexican economy even faster along a very different path. In the first case, authoritarian rule in Mexico worked against U.S. interests; in the second case, it worked to their benefit. Whether either case served Mexico's own interests remains an actively debated topic within Mexico.

President Salinas's decision to seek a free trade agreement with the United States coincided with a similar decision by President Bush with regard to Mexico. The U.S. president understood that the world was organizing itself into regional trade blocs. For the U.S. economy to remain globally competitive, the United States needed to strengthen its economic ties with Latin America, where it had a comparative advantage. The place to start was Mexico, where the Salinas reforms had enhanced Mexico's chances of becoming a dynamic market for U.S. investment and exports. In addition, a free trade agreement with Mexico would help that country's economic reformers consolidate their reforms. The Bush administration regarded this outcome as beneficial to both Mexico and the United States.

The Bush administration's support for Mexico's economic opening was not paralleled by support for an equivalent political opening. Washington agreed with President Salinas's argument that to simultaneously open the economy and the political system would weaken both types of reforms. Stated differently, President Bush accepted President Salinas's claim that perestroika had to precede glasnost if the Mexican president were to avoid the fate of Soviet president Mikhail Gorbachev and have sufficient power and authority to successfully modernize the Mexican economy. The last thing that the United States wanted was an unstable Mexico on its border. The existence in Mexico of a modern, reform-minded president who valued a close and cooperative relationship with the United States was the best that Washington could have hoped for as Mexico tried to put itself back on its feet. Furthermore, it is rarely if ever U.S. policy to press for democratic reform in a country before its citizens strongly and actively demand it. In its support for democratic transitions in nondemocratic countries, Washington usually waits until the nondemocratic ruler has become very unpopular or is pursuing policies that severely threaten U.S. interests before signaling more explicitly its support for a democratic transition. Such was not yet the situation in Mexico during the Salinas administration.

The emphasis on economic issues during the Bush and Salinas administrations did not mean that the more traditional bilateral issues had disappeared from the U.S.-Mexico agenda. Drugs and illegal immigration remained problematic, especially in view of the deteriorating living standards in Mexico resulting from the economic crisis and the stabilization policies implemented to deal with it. The United States, however, purposely chose to de-link the various issues in the bilateral relationship rather than use its leverage in one area to force Mexican compliance or agreement in another. The most important U.S. goal was a good working relationship with the Salinas government. The Mexican government shared this priority and refrained from attacking Washington, behavior that had been common during the 1970s in order to shore up political support at home.

President Bush left office having successfully negotiated a free trade agreement with Mexico but before the agreement had been approved by Congress. It fell to his Democratic successor, Bill Clinton, to win congressional support for NAFTA. He was able to do so with the help of a substantial number of Republican votes and by agreeing to incorporate protection for labor and the environment into side agreements, which won him the support of an important number of Democratic lawmakers.

By the end of 1993, therefore, there was reason for optimism concerning U.S.-Mexican relations. A complicated trade agreement involving both Mexico and Canada had been successfully negotiated and was about to be implemented. Mexico had made impressive progress in stabilizing, restructuring, and opening its economy. In the process, trade between the United States and Mexico had more than doubled, to the mutual benefit of both countries. There was also a notable increase in cooperation in the fight against illegal immigration and drug trafficking. Unfortunately, appearances were deceiving. January 1, 1994, would go down in history not only as the day that NAFTA took effect, but also as the first day of a year that in Mexico would be marked by political and economic crisis.

New Forces Shaping Bilateral Relations

With the benefit of hindsight, the political and economic turmoil that engulfed Mexico during NAFTA's first year should have come as no surprise. Mexico's authoritarian political system, which had traditionally concentrated great power in the presidency, had allowed President Salinas to undertake a highly ambitious project of economic reform despite important opposition from groups whose interests would be adversely affected, at least in the short run. The Mexican president, however, had believed that the rapid implementation of the agreement would be so good for Mexico that within a short period NAFTA would have enough domestic support to survive its opponents' attacks. What Salinas did not foresee was the strength of opposition to the agreement within the United States, due in part to an economic recession and in part to the defeat of a pro–free trade Republican president by a Democrat who had been supported by organized labor and other groups opposed to NAFTA. Although President Clinton was ultimately able to win support for the agreement, the process took longer than President Salinas had anticipated. The delay gave opponents of his economic reforms valuable time to organize.

In the past, active opposition to a sitting president had been an extremely risky undertaking in Mexico, given the president's vast powers and the resources at his disposal. By 1994, however, the situation had changed significantly. The very economic reforms that President Salinas had risked so much to implement, such as the privatization of state enterprises and the reduction of the state's role in the economy, had deprived him of the tools and resources he needed to keep disgruntled opponents of his reforms in line. His problems were further exacerbated by the implementation of NAFTA, which gave these groups the unprecedented opportunity to pressure the Mexican government by appealing to U.S. opponents of the agreement.

Stated differently, Mexico's economic opening, combined with the greater interdependence between Mexico and the United States, changed the balance of power within Mexico. The reforms weakened the Mexican presidency at the same time that NAFTA blurred the line between domestic and foreign policies in Mexico. This line had always been somewhat blurred, of course, given the overwhelming economic and military power of the United States. But with NAFTA, Mexican opponents of Salinas's reforms were able to join forces with U.S. opponents of the free trade agreement in order to apply unprecedented pressure on a president whose powers and freedom of action had become progressively diminished.

This helps to explain Salinas's apparent loss of political control in 1994. On January 1, a new armed guerrilla group made its presence known in Chiapas, to the surprise of many people in both Mexico and the United States who had come to believe that Mexico was fast becoming a First World country. After attempting an armed response, the government changed course and spent the better part of the year locked in negotiations with the guerrillas. In March, the PRI's presidential candidate was brutally assassinated, thereby casting doubt on the country's ability to hold elections in July as well as to decide them honestly if they were held. The selection of Ernesto Zedillo Ponce de León, a man who was regarded as more of a technocrat than a politician, did not inspire confidence among people in Mexico and abroad who felt that the times called for an experienced and strong leader. Mexico's political instability also began to generate fears regarding the economy, which had become heavily dependent on foreign short-term capital in order to sustain the reform process. That, combined with fears of an impending devaluation, accelerated capital flight. The new Zedillo administration, in office less than a month, decided to devalue the peso. The decision and its inept handling triggered a run on the currency, undermining investor confidence not only in Mexico but throughout Latin America and other emerging markets.

The ensuing economic crisis in Mexico would have involved the United States even if NAFTA had not existed. NAFTA, however, had raised the U.S. stake in the Mexican economy considerably. In fact, it had made Mexico as much a domestic policy issue for the United States as the United States had traditionally been for Mexico. It leveled the playing field between Mexico and the United States by broadening the number of groups in the United States who had come to believe that their interests could be affected by developments in Mexico.

The Bailout Decision

The so-called bailout decision therefore became the first clear post-NAFTA example of Mexico's enhanced impact on U.S. domestic politics. President Clinton, with the cooperation of the Republican heads of the House and Senate, quickly decided that the United States had to support the peso with a multi-billion-dollar rescue package. The U.S. Congress, however, refused to cooperate. The administration then shifted to a joint executive branch–IMF (International Monetary Fund) rescue package, based on the Treasury Department's Stabilization Fund, to provide Mexico with the necessary funds.

The coalition of forces that opposed the Mexican bailout was basically the same one that had opposed NAFTA one year earlier. Ross Perot and his supporters had argued during the NAFTA debates that Mexico would devalue its currency after the agreement took effect in order to gain a competitive advantage vis-à-vis the United States; they now claimed vindication. They were joined by the same environmental, human rights, and pro-democracy groups that earlier had opposed signing a free trade agreement until Mexico's record in these areas had significantly improved. In addition, organized labor, which had argued that NAFTA would destroy U.S. companies and jobs, was now joined by the newly elected

Republicans in Congress, who were considerably less committed to free trade than their Republican predecessors had been. Other opponents of the bailout included anti–Wall Street populists who argued that U.S. investors rather than U.S. taxpayers should pay the bill for Mexico's rescue.

The pro-NAFTA coalition was unable to prevail this time around because the rescue package was so intimately linked by its opponents to NAFTA. Pro-NAFTA groups had originally argued that the agreement would create employment both in Mexico and the United States, that the Mexican government would not devalue the peso, and that Mexico's transition to an industrial democracy would be aided by NAFTA. Less than one year after NAFTA's implementation, the treaty's opponents could turn their arguments against these groups. All efforts by the administration to de-link NAFTA and the bailout issue failed, even though an argument could be, and was, made that the devaluation was more the result of bad economic policymaking and electoral considerations in Mexico than of NAFTA. Furthermore, the claim that it was in the U.S. national interest to have a stable Mexico as a neighbor did not resonate nearly as much as bread-and-butter domestic concerns, such as unemployment and the use of taxpayer dollars to help a foreign country during a period of economic recession at home.

It is impossible to know whether Mexico ultimately avoided economic collapse because of the bailout, since the nonbailout scenario was never put to a test. It is also difficult to know what impact Mexico's failure to repay the U.S. Treasury would have had on U.S.-Mexican relations and specifically on the future of NAFTA, although it would not have been good. As it turned out, in January 1997 Mexico repaid the remaining U.S.$3.5 billion of the U.S.$13.5 billion it had borrowed from the United States, thereby undermining the dire prophecies of the bailout's opponents and depriving them of some ammunition for future attacks on NAFTA. Unfortunately, there was no shortage of issues involving U.S. relations with Mexico on which to mobilize the anti-NAFTA coalition.

The Immigration Issue

The degree to which NAFTA had blurred the line between domestic and foreign policies regarding Mexico became particularly apparent during 1995, when immigration became a contentious issue that threatened to undermine President Clinton's reelection efforts. One month before the Mexican devaluation, California's voters had approved Proposition 187, which blocked illegal immigrants' access to education, welfare, and nonemergency health services.

Supporters of the measure argued that the financial burden of pay-
ing for these services for illegals, who were mainly Mexican, had
become too great and that the benefits themselves were encouraging
the influx of even more illegal immigrants into the state. There was
some truth to this view, although it was also true that many
Californians were benefiting from the inexpensive labor provided
by the illegal immigrants. Nevertheless, California was at the
time experiencing a deep economic recession, as a result of military
base closings, the downsizing of defense contractors in the aftermath of the Cold War, and efforts to reduce the size of state government and increase California's global competitivenesss. These
developments magnified the costs to Californians of illegal immigration.

The implementation of Proposition 187 was ultimately delayed
by lawsuits filed against it, but the immigration issue was embraced
by Pat Buchanan in his bid for the 1996 Republican presidential
nomination. After Buchanan's victory in the New Hampshire primary in February 1996, other Republican candidates hardened their
positions on both illegal and legal immigration. President Clinton
felt obligated to do the same, given his desire to win not only
California's fifty-four electoral votes, but the thirty-two of Texas and
the twenty-five of Florida as well. Early in the campaign, he therefore urged revision of the extremely liberal policy that allowed more
than one million new legal immigrants into the United States annually. He also proposed legislation to increase the budget of the
Immigration and Naturalization Service (INS) from U.S.$2.1 billion
to U.S.$2.6 billion, which enabled the INS to place more border
patrol agents, inspectors, and investigators along the U.S.-Mexico
border. Efforts by some congressmen to restrict the entry of and benefits for legal immigrants were successfully resisted, in part because
of strong lobbying by U.S. business leaders who said such action
would hurt their ability to hire skilled foreign workers.

The new legislation, which took effect in April 1997, stiffens the
requirements for granting political asylum, makes it easier for immigration authorities to deport arriving foreigners, and makes it harder to win a waiver of a deportation decision. It also requires all illegal immigrants to leave the United States within six months of their
arrival in the United States and bars most of them from returning for
at least several years.

In order to avoid deportation, large numbers of Mexicans living
illegally in the United States rushed to apply for U.S. citizenship
before the law took effect. The widespread panic that the law generated had an impact on U.S.-Mexico bilateral relations because

Mexican government officials took issue with the treatment of Mexican citizens living illegally in the United States. At about the same time, however, Mexico passed a constitutional amendment allowing Mexicans to adopt U.S. citizenship without losing their rights as Mexicans. The Mexican government apparently believed that allowing Mexican citizens to become U.S. citizens would enable Mexico to better defend its interests in the United States. Finally, the fact that the impetus behind the more stringent U.S. immigration laws had come from the Republican party encouraged an overwhelming majority of the new Mexican-American citizens to register as Democrats.

It is evident from the way the immigration issue was discussed and dealt with in the United States that it was viewed primarily as a domestic issue rather than a foreign policy one, despite the fact that it was consistently linked with the Mexican devaluation and with NAFTA. The fact that 358,000 arrests were made by the border patrol during the first quarter of 1995, compared with 276,000 in the first quarter of 1994, did indeed establish a link between Mexico's economic crisis and the increase in illegal immigration. It did not, however, necessarily tie the immigration issue to NAFTA, as some anti-immigration groups argued. Once again, however, the NAFTA issue helped shape the debate on illegal immigration from Mexico and broadened domestic opposition within the United States to the entry of Mexicans, whether legal or illegal.

The Drug Issue

As a result of successful efforts by the U.S. Drug Enforcement Agency to reduce shipments of drugs from South America to Florida and the Atlantic seaboard, the Colombian drug cartels began trans-shipping drugs through Mexico instead. Subsequently, Mexican criminals established their own distribution networks and territories independent of the Colombian cartels. As a result, an estimated 75 percent of the cocaine entering the United States now arrives from Mexico. In addition, Mexican criminals also moved large amounts of heroin and marijuana across the border into the United States.

Mexico's contribution to the U.S. drug problem quickly became a campaign issue when in March 1996 President Clinton had to decide whether the Mexican government was cooperating enough with U.S. antinarcotics programs. If it was not, the president would have had to recommend that Congress decertify the country, thereby making Mexico ineligible for several aid programs and running the risk of endangering bilateral cooperation on a variety of other issues, as well as possibly undermining Mexico's still fragile economic recovery. Sensitive to the increased domestic pressures facing President Clinton in an election year, Mexican authorities arrested Juan García Abrego, a notorious drug lord, and expelled him to the United States. This helped Clinton argue that Mexico was cooperating with the U.S. antidrug effort and therefore should not be decertified. The administration simultaneously recommended that Colombia be decertified, given the absence of presidential cooperation in that country.

Clinton's decision on Mexico prompted Senators Alphonse D'Amato (R., N.Y.) and Dianne Feinstein (D., Calif.) to introduce legislation to block additional economic help to Mexico if it did not do more to stop the entry of illegal drugs into the United States. D'Amato had been one of the most vocal opponents of the Mexican bailout, whereas Feinstein, who planned to run for governor of California, had opposed NAFTA and had pressed for tougher immigration laws in order to halt the inflow of undocumented Mexicans into her state. Ultimately, Congress supported the president and certified Mexico, but his victory was only temporary. When Mexico had to be certified again in 1997, opponents of certification found themselves in a considerably stronger position.

Throughout 1996 evidence of the involvement of high-ranking Mexican officials with the drug cartels had continued to surface. Some of the most notorious information concerned Mario Ruiz Massieu, the former coordinator of Mexico's antidrug effort in 1993–1994, who was in U.S. custody. There were also growing indications that the jailed Raul Salinas de Gortari, the brother of the former Mexican president, had used his power and connections to protect drug shipments and traffickers. Two incumbent Mexican governors were also reportedly in league with the cartels. But the biggest blow to the Clinton administration's case in favor of again certifying Mexico was the arrest in February 1997 of Jesús Gutiérrez Rebollo, a Mexican army general who had been appointed Mexico's drug czar only two months earlier.

The arrest of Gutiérrez Rebollo severely embarrassed General Barry McCaffery, the U.S. drug czar. In December 1996 McCaffery had praised the Mexican general as "a man of tremendous courage and integrity."[1] The Gutiérrez Rebollo situation also made it difficult for the Clinton administration to argue that the Mexican government was cooperating with Washington in the fight against drug trafficking, particularly since the Mexican government had not warned Washington of the impending arrest of Gutiérrez Rebollo. Furthermore, the case called into question the desirability of drug cooperation with Mexico, since Washington had shared sensitive information with Gutiérrez Rebollo, which obviously had been compromised. The fact that the Mexican general was the third top Mexican drug enforcement official to be implicated in drug corruption heightened this concern.

The Mexican government argued that the arrest of Gutiérrez Rebollo was proof that Mexico was committed to fighting drug traffickers. This was true but insufficient to allow Clinton to pursue his decision to have Mexico certified. Shortly before the March 1, 1997, deadline for certification, therefore, Washington presented the Mexican government with a list of drug-related issues on which the United States needed to see some action by Mexico. The issues included the extradition of drug traffickers and increased prosecution under Mexico's new money laundering and organized crime laws. Apparently satisfied that the Zedillo administration would take the necessary action, Clinton proceeded to recommend that Mexico be certified, while again arguing against comparable certification for Colombia, which in the eyes of many had in fact done more than Mexico over the past year to combat drug traffickers.

Less than two weeks after Clinton certified Mexico, the House voted to overrule his decision by a vote of 251 to 175. The anticertification campaign was led in the Senate by Dianne Feinstein and in the House of Representatives by Richard Gephardt (D., Mo.), leader of the anti-NAFTA forces. The margin was insufficient to allow Congress to overturn an anticipated presidential veto. Shortly thereafter, the Senate voted 94 to 5 in favor of upholding the certification of Mexico but required Clinton to issue a special report on Mexico's drug policy efforts, including progress in eradicating corruption within the Mexican government, by September 1.

Mexico responded to the campaign to decertify its drug cooperation efforts by arguing that the entire decertification process was an affront to Mexican sovereignty and pointing out once again that real progress against drug traffickers would prove elusive as long as the United States continued to consume such large quantities of drugs. Mexico also warned that decertification would make it impossible for Mexico to continue to cooperate with the United States in the fight against drugs. The government, however, acknowledged that it had a problem by dismantling its old antidrug force and creating a new, more independent agency modeled after the U.S. Drug Enforcement Agency. Its members would be subjected to a series of drug, polygraph, and other tests to attest to their reliability before being hired. Such screening of drug officials was new for Mexico.

The drug issue is a good example of how both the United States and Mexico are constrained in their behavior in one issue area because of the larger bilateral relationship. Despite strong evidence of the involvement of high-ranking Mexican officials with drug traffickers, Clinton feared that decertification of Mexico could undermine that country's economic recovery and strengthen forces in Mexico that opposed the economic reforms as well as the closer economic integration with the United States that resulted from them. On the Mexican side, the government risked alienating foreign investors and thereby aborting its successful economic recovery efforts by doing nothing in reaction to growing evidence of high-level official involvement with drug traffickers.

Perhaps equally important for the first time was the power of public opinion within Mexico. The greater freedom of the press, combined with stronger opposition parties, was making the Mexican government more accountable for its behavior. High-level corruption was fast becoming an electoral issue as Mexico approached the critical July 1997 midterm elections. As a result of a series of electoral reforms, there was a growing possibility that the PRI could lose control of Congress. The economic reforms had led to accelerated political reform, which in turn was making the government less secretive and more accountable to its own people. On the drug issue, the accountability cut two ways. On the one hand, Mexican government officials had to be seen within Mexico as protecting Mexican sovereignty against U.S. efforts to tell it what to do. On the other hand, they also were being held accountable by the Mexican people, who had become less tolerant of official corruption as it had become increasingly exposed.

NAFTA Issues

The other major issue in U.S.-Mexican relations that surfaced during the 1996 presidential campaign involved NAFTA, specifically the implementation of a provision involving cross-border trucking. According to the agreement, states along the border were to open to foreign trucks on December 18, 1995. The U.S. government, however, decided unilaterally to ban Mexican trucks from roads in Texas, New Mexico, Arizona, and California because of "safety worries." Although there were undoubtedly some legitimate safety concerns, these could have been dealt with on a case-by-case basis. The decision clearly had less to do with safety than with politics. Specifically, the Clinton administration wanted to avoid alienating the powerful Teamsters Union, which opposed the opening out of fears that they would not be able to compete with lower-paid Mexican truckers.

Also relevant was the desire not to antagonize important groups of voters in the border states where anti-Mexican sentiment was running high. The administration's unilateral trucking decision was therefore aimed at avoiding the mobilization of the broad opposition coalition that had played an active role in U.S.-Mexican issues since the NAFTA debates. By mid-1997, the trucking issue had not been resolved.

Interestingly, the Mexican government also was less than forceful in pressing for compliance with the trucking provisions of NAFTA because many Mexican truckers were afraid that they would be unable to compete with U.S. truckers, whose vehicles were more sophisticated and who were better organized.

Another NAFTA issue, which in fact became a nonissue during the presidential campaign, involved the expansion of NAFTA to include Chile. Ever since NAFTA's creation, Washington had been promising Chile, with its open markets and democratic political system, that it would be next in line. In order to implement that promise, the U.S. Congress had to extend fast-track authority, which would limit votes on trade agreements to a yes or no vote, with no amendments possible. Following Mexico's devaluation of the peso, however, it became a political liability to talk about expanding NAFTA, and the odds of obtaining enough votes to pass fast-track legislation in 1996 were nil. As a result, the Clinton administration opted to postpone consideration of Chile's accession to NAFTA until after the November 1996 elections.

It was not until September 1997, however, that the administration submitted fast-track legislation to Congress. It claimed that the delay was due to the need to deal first with the U.S. budget and the issue of granting most-favored-nation status to China. Although supporters of fast-track criticized the delay, it is doubtful that Congress would have voted in favor of expanding NAFTA as long as anti-Mexico sentiment remained high and before the "report card" on NAFTA was submitted by the administration to Congress in July 1997. Furthermore, it made sense for the president to delay the fast-track debate to give the Mexican economy more time to recover.

As it turned out, the NAFTA report proved inconclusive. The administration noted the difficulties of isolating the effect of NAFTA on the U.S. economy but claimed that it had had "a modest positive effect on U.S. net exports, income, investment and jobs supported by exports."[2] Mexico's tariffs had dropped from about 10 percent to under 3 percent because of NAFTA. Imports from the United States had grown from 69 percent of total Mexican imports to 75 percent by 1996. The report attributed the even larger increase in Mexican exports to the United States during the same period to the strength of the U.S. economy rather than to NAFTA. Although U.S. employment grew by almost 8.6 million jobs during the first three years of NAFTA, the report could not conclusively attribute such growth to NAFTA. The Labor Department also released data showing that there were 99,500 layoffs attributable to NAFTA in its first three years. Because the rules to qualify for benefits do not require proving that NAFTA was the cause of a worker's layoff, the data are not reliable. In fact, pro-NAFTA people have noted that of the 99,500 workers who have been certified as eligible for trade-adjustment assistance, only 12,200 have actually applied for the benefits. This suggested, they argued, that some of the dismissed workers had been rehired. And as one analyst pointed out, "The United States has created as many new jobs every two weeks as have been documented to be lost because of imports from Canada and Mexico over the entire existence of NAFTA."[3]

The inconclusive correlation between NAFTA and job loss or gain, however, was offset in part by the spectacular recovery of both the U.S. and Mexican economies. Much of the anti-NAFTA sentiment had coincided with an economic recession in the United States. This was also a period in which the U.S. economy was undergoing a profound restructuring in order to increase its global competitiveness. California, an important anti-NAFTA state, had been badly hit by both developments. By mid-1997, however, the signs of a booming U.S. economy were clear, and California's economy was growing rapidly. Economic data from Mexico told a similar story, which is not surprising given Mexico's interdependence with the U.S. economy. In 1996, Mexico's gross domestic product (GDP) grew by 5.1 percent, whereas in 1997 the economy was projected to grow by more than 6.0 percent, with second-quarter growth to reach 8.8 percent.

The impressive economic growth in the United States and Mexico (as well as in Canada) during the first several years of NAFTA translated into important increases in U.S.-Mexican trade. Mexico replaced Japan as the second-most-important U.S. trading partner during this period. By the end of 1997, bilateral trade was expected to reach U.S.$160 billion, or twice the amount of U.S.-Mexican trade in 1993, before NAFTA. Furthermore, forty-four out of fifty U.S. states increased their export sales to Mexico in 1996 compared with 1995. NAFTA's opponents, however, focused their attention on the import side, where the United States did have a $16 billion deficit in merchandise trade with Mexico in 1996 and an even larger deficit of $23 billion with Canada. At the same time, however, the very fact that Mexico was able to increase its exports to the U.S. market during its economic crisis clearly was crucial to its ability to revive its economy in such a relatively short period of time.

The results of NAFTA, therefore, give ammunition to both sides. The Clinton administration's decision to postpone asking for fast-track authority until 1997 was a wise decision because of the extremely broad-based and strong opposition to NAFTA and the anti-Mexico sentiments that existed through 1996. On the other hand, the administration's failure to reach a compromise with those Democrats who wanted to include labor and environmental protections in the legislation and those Republicans who wanted trade legislation to deal only with trade ultimately led to Congress' refusal to give the president fast-track authority.

It is likely nonetheless that NAFTA will be expanded and deepened in the coming years. Because NAFTA is a free trade agreement, there is no legal requirement for Mexico, the United States, and Canada to coordinate their fiscal and monetary policies or to adopt similar procedures in areas such as customs. As the integration of the three North American economies continues to increase, however, it seems inevitable that all three parties to the agreement will find it necessary to adopt similar kinds of rules and procedures; at some point, for example, the three countries might decide to discuss exchange rate coordination or even the possible adoption of a single North American currency or a single legal system. Given the overwhelming size of the U.S. economy compared to that of Mexico, there is little doubt that if these issues were ever to receive serious consideration, the United States, not Mexico, would set the standard. Whether this situation would prove acceptable to Mexico (and Canada) remains to be seen. Whatever the ultimate decision, it will be preceded by much debate and hard bargaining, which will cause additional volatility in the U.S.-Mexico relationship.

Although NAFTA, immigration, and drugs constitute the key issues in the U.S. relationship with Mexico, the fact that they are increasingly viewed through a domestic rather than a foreign policy prism was neatly summed up when both the Democratic and Republican candidates were criticized for ignoring foreign policy issues during the campaign. This accusation was made despite the considerable discussion and debate during the campaign focusing on U.S.-Mexican issues such as immigration, drugs, and NAFTA. The blurring of the line will increase even more with Mexico's accelerated transition toward democratic government.

Mexico's Democratic Transition

The July 1997 midterm elections in Mexico marked a turning point in Mexico's transition to democracy. When the votes were counted, the PRI had lost control of the lower house of Congress for the first time in its history. Given the powers of the lower house in deciding on appropriations and spending as well as its power to investigate alleged wrongdoing by government officials, the PRI's loss of congressional control signaled important changes in how domestic policy was to be made, with implications for Mexico's relations with the United States.

In addition, Cuauhtémoc Cárdenas, a founding leader of the left-of-center Party of the Democratic Revolution (PRD), had become the first elected mayor of Mexico City, the country's largest city with a population of 16 million. Cárdenas's victory immediately enhanced his chances of becoming the PRD's presidential candidate in the elections in the year 2000 and possibly winning the election to become Mexico's first opposition president since 1929. Given Washington's many years of working with PRI presidents, such a possibility also implied important changes in U.S.-Mexican relations.

Mexico's democratic transition did not, of course, begin in 1997. In fact, it was a long time coming and reflects a series of electoral reforms implemented since the 1960s as well as changes in Mexican society that include urbanization, the growth of the middle class, and the spread of modern technology and communications. But perhaps the most important force for democracy in recent years was Mexico's economic reform project, which weakened the power of the state and increased the influence of global economic and political forces on Mexico, particularly those emanating from the United States.

An early example of how this process worked involved NAFTA. Opponents of Mexico's economic reforms and of the free trade agreement discovered that they had new leverage against the Mexican government by virtue of their ability to incite or report on behavior that would provide ammunition to NAFTA's foes in the United States. Middle-class intellectuals and others who had grown increasingly disenchanted with the PRI's policy failures and government corruption and the absence of democracy in Mexico also came to appreciate the new leverage that their government's desire to see NAFTA approved inadvertently gave them. The anti-NAFTA forces and the pro-democracy ones overlapped to some extent in their desire to see an end to the PRI's dominance.

The anti-NAFTA groups were not able to keep Mexico out of NAFTA because the PRI controlled both houses of Congress until the July 1997 elections. They were, however, able to wrest a number of political concessions from the government both before, but especially after, NAFTA was approved because opposition to the agreement remained strong in the United States. It became even stronger following the peso devaluation of December 1994, which created fear among U.S. workers that they would lose their jobs during a time of recession in the United States to much-lower-paid Mexican workers. Since Mexico needed U.S. support to avoid a financial collapse, as well as NAFTA's continued existence to allow its export-led economic recovery to continue, the Mexican government felt obliged to agree to a number of important political reforms that slowly began to level the playing field between the PRI and the opposition parties.

One of the most important reforms was the creation of an entity independent of both the government and the PRI to ensure the honest administration of the 1997 midterm elections and an accurate count of the votes. Also important was the decision to provide government funding to all political parties fielding candidates in the election. Although the funds were not distributed equally to all the parties, for the first time the opposition parties had access to substantial sums of money with which to organize and buy television time. The new reforms also provided for television to give equal coverage to the candidates. In the past, coverage of the PRI candidate had been overwhelming, with news about the opposition candidates either lacking or purposely biased against them. Finally, various steps were taken, beginning with the presidential election of 1994 when the government was trying to win over U.S. opponents of NAFTA, that made it more difficult to tamper with the vote, including the issuance of sophisticated, high-tech voter identification cards with photos and a computerized fingerprint chip; transparent ballot boxes; and the presence of representatives of opposition parties during the voting and vote count. In the 1994 elections the government also began to allow foreign observers to witness the voting in order to help ensure its fairness and honesty. In the past, the government had strongly resisted such foreign involvement on the grounds that it constituted an infringement on Mexico's sovereignty. Opposition groups had supported the government's position, in part out of nationalist or anti-American sentiment and in part because to oppose the government's stance at that time seemed risky. By 1994, and especially by 1997, the opposition had changed its mind.

One final new element that contributed to Mexico's accelerated move to democracy was U.S. policy. Washington's top priority has long been a stable and friendly Mexico on its southern border. For most of the period since 1929, when the PRI was established under a different name, the existence of a dominant political party that controlled the presidency and, until fairly recently, all state governorships, was viewed by Washington as in the interests of both Mexico and the United States, despite the fact that the Mexican government's foreign policy was often critical of U.S. policy toward Mexico and the rest of Latin America. In a sense, there was a tacit agreement between Mexico and the United States to disagree. Although Mexico's leftist foreign policy sometimes caused problems for Washington, particularly with regard to the Castro government in Cuba and the Central American conflict in the 1980s, at the same time it allowed a series of Mexican presidents to win support from left-wing political groups and intellectuals within Mexico, thereby enhancing the government's legitimacy and stability at home.

Given the high priority it placed on a stable and friendly Mexico, the promotion of democracy in Mexico was not an important element of Washington's policy toward Mexico. During the Cold War in particular, the United States had no desire to press the PRI to democratize, since such behavior could easily have brought to power a government that would have been further to the left than the PRI and considerably more friendly to countries hostile to the United States. The policy did not change much in the late 1980s and early 1990s, when President Salinas chose to liberalize Mexico's economy while keeping democratic reforms to a minimum. The U.S. government, in fact, generally accepted Salinas's argument that Mexico could not undertake economic and political reforms simultaneously, since the government needed to use the power of the authoritarian political system to make major and necessary economic changes in the absence of a popular consensus favoring them.

Washington did take note, however, of the growing economic policymaking failures of successive Mexican administrations beginning with the presidency of Echeverría and accelerating with the administration of López Portillo. Furthermore, as Mexico's population became wealthier and better-educated, elements of its growing middle class began to intensify their criticism of authoritarian rule and press for a more pluralistic, participatory, and accountable form of government. Slowly, U.S. government officials in both Washington and Mexico began to broaden their contacts and communication with other political party leaders, spokespersons of the rapidly increasing nongovernmental organizations, and state and local government officials from opposition parties on the right and left.

The end of the Cold War in 1989 removed the main obstacle to Washington's ability to accept with relative equanimity a democratic transition in Mexico (and other Latin American countries) that could bring to power a left-of-center president. Its changed attitude coincided with a growing pro-democracy movement on the part of Mexicans themselves. The most obvious signal of Washington's ability to accept and work with a non-PRI government, whether of the right or left, was given during President Clinton's visit to Mexico in May 1997. For the first time an incumbent U.S. president met formally with the leaders of Mexico's left-wing and right-wing opposition parties. The meetings gave enhanced domestic and international legitimacy to the opposition parties and probably helped them maintain the momentum that cost the PRI its majority in the lower house of Congress, as well as its control of the government of Mexico City.

There is no certainty, of course, that the opposition's victories in the July 1997 midterm elections mean that the PRI's candidate in the presidential elections of 2000 will lose. The PRI still has the largest and best-functioning political machine, with a presence in urban and rural areas throughout the country. The National Action Party (PAN), in contrast, is only well organized in the north and in one or two other states. The PRD has the weakest organization, although the party's strong showing in the 1997 congressional elections and the election of Cuauhtémoc Cárdenas as mayor of Mexico City may encourage more Mexicans, including those from the left wing of the PRI who are unhappy with the liberal economic reforms made by a series of PRI presidents, to become active members of the party. But if an opposition candidate were to win the presidential elections of 2000, there is no doubt that Washington would seek and welcome a good working relationship with the new president and his team.

In the meantime, the PRI's loss of control of Congress will have important implications for U.S.-Mexican relations. At the very least, the bilateral relationship will become more difficult to manage. Until now, the greater complexity and policy incoherence was on the U.S. side, since the president and the Congress did not necessarily agree on policy toward Mexico. Furthermore, within Congress there was often conflict over U.S. policy toward Mexico, not only between the Democratic and Republican parties but also within each party. In Mexico, there was also disagreement expressed in Congress on a variety of issues involving the United States. Nevertheless, until very recently, the PRI's control of Congress, combined with the power of the presidency, helped Mexico speak more or less with one voice on bilateral issues.

Such unity will no longer be the case. The Mexican Congress has become considerably more pluralistic in the aftermath of the July 1997 elections. Furthermore, the PRI's defeat has widened the division within the PRI between the so-called reformers, who support the economic opening, NAFTA, and Mexico's democratic transition, and the so-called dinosaurs, composed of the PRI's old guard. The latter continue to harbor strong doubts about the wisdom and desirability of NAFTA; believe that the state's role in the economy must be strengthened; and have a certain nostalgia for some of the traditional, more authoritarian ways of doing things.

As a result of these changes, the Mexican Congress will now behave more like the U.S. Congress on bilateral issues, sometimes supporting the president and at other times fighting to block his legislative initiatives. Like the United States, Mexico will also speak with more than one main voice regarding its policy toward the United States, and just as the multiple U.S. voices were often confusing and even offensive to many Mexicans, the many Mexican voices will now confuse and offend U.S. citizens from time to time.

It is even possible that politics in Mexico may appear more unstable and threatening to U.S. (and possibly Mexican) interests. The conventional wisdom is that the basic economic reforms that Mexico has implemented over the last decade are here to stay, in part because the leaders of all of Mexico's main political parties have concluded that there is no escaping the need to operate within the new global economy and, also, because there is no perceived alternative to the new policies. Although the conventional wisdom is probably correct, at least with regard to the leadership of Mexico's main parties, there are already signs that the position of the rank-and-file members is somewhat different. Furthermore, it remains unclear how much control the PRI, PRD, and PAN leaders have over their followers. At the very least, Mexico's policymaking processes will not move in a straight line. Instead, there will probably be some steps forward followed by a step back, at least until the main political parties work out the terms of their support for the reform process.

All of this means that the next several years will see unprecedented debate and discussion over Mexico's domestic and foreign policies, including those relating to the United States. The U.S. government and its citizens will have to learn how to sort out what is really important from what is not and act accordingly, which is essentially what the Mexican government and its citizens have had to do vis-à-vis the U.S. policymaking process. The new congruence between the two countries' policymaking processes will probably lead to the modification or elimination of some of the more needless-ly offensive behavior or policies on the U.S. side. The drug certifica-tion process is a likely candidate, since the costs of the certification process, in terms of U.S. relations with Mexico, have come to out-weigh its perceived benefits.

If greater democracy in Mexico will make U.S.-Mexico relations even harder to manage, it will also help ensure that the reform process, assuming it continues, will have greater staying power because it will have broader popular support. At the same time, a more democratic Mexico should be better able to understand and accept the untidiness that has long characterized the making of U.S. policy toward Mexico. In addition, on the U.S. side, the anti-Mexico public opinion, which was linked in part to the absence of democra-cy in Mexico, should also begin to diminish. Both developments will lead to a more mature and cooperative bilateral relationship in the coming years, to the benefit of both countries.

Notes

1. "U.S. Ex-General Lavish in Praising Mexican Allies in Drug War," *New York Times*, December 12, 1996, p. A19.

2. Clinton administration's report to Congress on the operations and effects of NAFTA, July 11, 1997, cited in *Oxford Analytica Daily Brief*, July 12, 1997.

3. Sidney Weintraub, *North American Free Trade and Investment Report* (Concord, Calif.: World Trade Executive, Inc., 1996), p. 9.

Appendix A

Chronology of Mexican History

1519   Hernán Cortés leads a Spanish expedition into Mexico. The Spaniards take the Aztec capital of Tenochtitlán in November.

1520   Permanent colonization of Nueva España begins.

1810   The movement for independence begins under the leadership of Miguel Hidalgo y Costilla.

1811   After Hidalgo's execution in July, José María Morelos assumes leadership of the independence movement.

1821   Independence from Spain is formally declared on February 24. The Treaty of Córdoba is signed on September 27, recognizing Mexican independence, but Spain fails to honor the agreement.

1822   The army of Agustín de Iturbide occupies Mexico City on May 18, and Iturbide declares himself emperor. His empire quickly crumbles, however, and the Republic of Mexico is founded by Antonio López de Santa Anna on December 1.

1824   The federal republican government is officially established under a new constitution. Guadalupe Victoria becomes the first president of Mexico.

1833   Santa Anna is elected president in December; he establishes his short-lived dictatorship in April of the following year.

1845   Texas is annexed by the United States.

1846   Mexico severs diplomatic relations with the United
            States, marking the beginning of the Mexican-American
            War (ending with the Treaty of Guadaloupe Hidalgo on
            February 2, 1848).

1857   The Constitution of 1857 is adopted on February 5.

1858   The War of the Reform begins, ending in 1860 with the
            triumph of Liberal forces over Conservative ones.

1861   Troops from Britain, France, and Spain land at Veracruz,
            in keeping with an agreement for intervention made
            among the three nations.

1863   The French conquer Puebla on May 17 and Mexico City
            on June 7.

1864   The reign of Ferdinand Maximilian Joseph (Emperor
            Maximilian) begins.

1867   Benito Juárez leads an offensive against Maximilian
            beginning in February. Juárez is elected president by
            December.

1876   Porfirio Díaz leads a rebellion, marking the beginning of
            his thirty-four-year tenure as Mexico's president/dicta-
            tor, known as the "Porfiriato." His regime becomes
            known for its slogan, "order and progress."

1910   In the year of Díaz's seventh reelection, rebellion breaks
            out in northern Mexico. Francisco I. Madero announces
            his *Plan of San Luis*, inviting Mexicans to rebel against
            the dictatorship under the slogan of "effective suffrage,
            no reelection."

1911   As rebellion spreads, Díaz resigns and is exiled to
            France. Francisco Madero assumes the presidency in
            October. Indian and peasant leader Emiliano Zapata
            publishes his *Plan of Ayala* in November, demanding
            broad reforms, especially in the area of land tenure.

1912   Pascual Orozco leads a rebellion against Madero, but the
            movement is crushed by the government forces of
            Victoriano Huerta. Huerta is exiled to France in July.
            Zapata and Francisco "Pancho" Villa occupy Mexico
            City in November. Venustiano Carranza establishes a
            constitutional government at Veracruz.

1913	Madero is overthrown in a coup led by Huerta and Félix Díaz and is subsequently assassinated. Zapata continues to lead rebellions in the south, while Carranza, Villa, and Álvaro Obregón remain powerful in the north. Huerta's government is dissolved in October.
1914	Huerta is defeated by U.S. troops in April and is forced into exile.
1915	Carranza is recognized by the United States as head of Mexican government forces.
1917	The Constitution of 1917 is promulgated, and Carranza is elected president.
1919	Zapata is assassinated.
1920	Obregón, after leading a rebellion this same year, is elected president following Carranza's death.
1923	Villa is assassinated.
1924	General Plutarco Elías Calles is elected president.
1928	Álvaro Obregón is reelected president but is assassinated shortly thereafter.
1929	The National Revolutionary Party (PNR), the official political party, is founded.
1934–1940	The presidency of Lázaro Cárdenas is characterized by socialist reforms, including the establishment of collective landholdings (*ejidos*) and the nationalization of the oil industry. The official government political party is renamed the Party of the Mexican Revolution (PRM).
1939	The National Action Party (PAN) is founded by Manuel Gómez Morín.
1940–1946	Manuel Ávila Camacho's administration initiates the process of import-substitution industrialization. He is the last military leader to hold the office of president.
1942	The PRM is reorganized and renamed the Institutional Revolutionary Party (PRI).
1946–1952	The administration of Miguel Alemán Valdés, the first civilian president of Mexico, is marked by a continued thrust toward industrialization.

1952–1958 Adolfo Ruiz Cortines, noted as a moderate and an administrator rather than a politician, undertakes austerity measures to regain control of the economy. The so-called stabilizing development model gains precedence, as growth under conditions of stability is the objective sought in the economic realm.

1958–1964 Following a rebellion by some of the nation's most important unions, former minister of labor Adolfo López Mateos ascends to the presidency. His tenure is characterized by increased private foreign investment in Mexico and control of the economy by foreign (especially U.S.) interests. His administration is also characterized by the implementation of land redistribution policies, increased agricultural production, and greater participation of minority parties in the political arena.

1964–1970 During Gustavo Díaz Ordaz's presidency, stabilizing development consolidates and reaches its full potential. Its limits also become apparent, however, as the government begins to face a major political crisis.

1968   Government forces attack protesting students on October 2, in what comes to be known as the Tlatelolco Massacre.

1970–1976 Under President Luis Echeverría Álvarez, stabilizing development becomes "shared development," which emphasizes a large state role in the economy and greater emphasis on distributive policies. Macroeconomic stability falters as inflation rises.

1976   The peso is devalued.

1976–1982 Following an initial period of austerity, President José López Portillo y Pacheco's economic policies come to rely more on populism than on reform. Shortly before the end of his term, the president announces the nationalization of private banks.

1978   Legislative reform introduces proportional representation into the Chamber of Deputies.

1981   Mexico becomes the world's fourth-largest producer of oil during the presidency of López Portillo.

1982   The peso is devalued as the nation faces an economic crisis. This marks the beginning of the so-called Latin American debt crisis.

1982–1988 President Miguel de la Madrid Hurtado immediately enacts austerity measures to combat the economic crisis. His administration is characterized by the government's ongoing struggle for "structural change" and adjustment.

1986 Petroleum prices crash. President de la Madrid signs Mexico on to the General Agreement on Tariffs and Trade (GATT).

1987 Political forces on the Mexican left converge to form the National Democratic Front (FDN). The FDN is a coalition of parties and other political organizations that formed to support Cuauhtémoc Cárdenas's candidacy for the 1988 presidential race.

1988–1994 After a highly competitive and disputed election Carlos Salinas de Gortari takes office. His administration is characterized by the "politics of modernization," which includes reducing the state's role in the economy, opening the economy, and fighting poverty.

1988 Ernesto Ruffo Appel, the first opposition party governor (a member of the PAN) is elected in Baja California.

1990 The Party of the Democratic Revolution (PRD) is founded.

1993 The North American Free Trade Agreement (NAFTA) is established between Mexico, Canada, and the United States.

1994 The day that NAFTA goes into effect (January 1), guerrillas of the Zapatista Army of National Liberation (EZLN) stage a major uprising in the southern state of Chiapas. A tentative peace accord is reached in March. Also in March, the PRI's presidential candidate, Luis Donaldo Colosio, is assassinated in Tijuana. The candidate chosen to replace him, Ernesto Zedillo Ponce de León, wins the August elections. On December 20 the peso is devalued by 15 percent, in the midst of Mexico's most dire economic crisis in recent history. The peso's value falls an additional 35 percent, for a total devaluation of 50 percent.

1995   U.S. president Bill Clinton approves a loan to Mexico to
            bail out the peso.

1997   In the July midterm elections, the PRI loses its majority
            in Congress for the first time since it was established.
            Cuauhtémoc Cárdenas of the PRD becomes the first
            elected mayor of the Federal District.

Appendix B

Study Group Sessions
and Participants

Gonzalo de Las Heras, group chairman
Susan Kaufman Purcell and Luis Rubio, group codirectors
Ross Culverwell, group rapporteur

Session 1 - March 2, 1994: "Coping with Political Change"
Commentator:
Luis Rubio, Director, Centro de Investigación para el Desarrollo,
A.C. (CIDAC), Mexico

Discussants:
Miguel Basáñez, President, MORI de México, Mexico
Federico Estévez, Dean of Social Sciences, Instituto Tecnológico
Autónomo de México (ITAM), Mexico
Alan Stoga, Managing Director, Kissinger Associates, New
York

Session 2 - April 12, 1994: "Crisis and Economic Change in Mexico"
Commentator:
Jesús Reyes Heroles, Director General, Grupo de Economistas y
Asociados (GEA), Mexico

Discussants:
Sergio Martín, Senior Economist, MACRO Asesoría Económica,
S.C., Mexico
Richard Weinert, President, Leslie, Weinert and Co., New York

Session 3 - May 23, 1994: "Poverty, Inequality, and the Politics of Welfare Reform"
Commentator:
Guillermo Trejo, Research Associate, Centro de Investigación para el Desarrollo, A.C. (CIDAC), Mexico; doctoral candidate, Columbia University, New York

Discussants:
José Casar, Director, Instituto Interamericano de Estudios Transnacionales (ILET), Mexico
Rolando Cordera, Director, NEXOS-TV, Mexico
Nora Lustig, Senior Fellow, Brookings Institution, Washington, D.C.

Session 4 - June 22, 1997: "The New U.S.-Mexico Relationship"
Commentator:
Susan Kaufman Purcell, Vice President, Americas Society, New York

Discussants:
George Grayson, Professor of Government, College of William and Mary, Virginia
Roberta Lajous, International Affairs Adviser, 1994 PRI Presidential Campaign, Mexico
Sergio Sarmiento, Chief Editor, *El Financiero Internacional*
Arturo Valenzuela, Deputy Assistant Secretary of State for Inter-American Affairs, U.S. Department of State, Washington, D.C.

Study Group Participants
David Asman, *Wall Street Journal*
John E. Avery, Americas Society
Charles Barber, former chairman of ASARCO
Jon Blum, Morgan Stanley and Company
Roberto Blum, Centro de Investigación para el Desarrollo, A.C. (CIDAC)
Jeffery Boetticher, Black Box Corporation
Ambassador Everett Ellis Briggs, Americas Society
Lars Christianson, Christianson S.A. de C.V.
Martin Coiteux, École des Hautes Études Commerciales (HEC)
Guy F. Erb, Goldman, Sachs and Co.
Rafael Fernández MacGregor, FEMAC, S.A.

Claudio X. González, Secretariat of Agriculture, Mexico
Jonathan E. Heath, MACRO Asesoría Económica, S.C.
Ruben Kraiem, Paul, Weiss, Rifkind, Wharton and Garrison
Marc Levinson, *Newsweek*
Javier Mora, United States–Mexico Chamber of Commerce
Martha T. Muse, Tinker Foundation
James M. Nash, Nomura Research
Roberto Newell, McKinsey and Company
Luis Niño de Rivera, Arrendadora Financiera Mexicana, S.A. de C.V.
Pablo Pascual Moncayo, Instituto de Estudios para la Transición Democrática
John E. Pearson, *Business Week*
Olga Pellicer, Instituto Tecnológico Autónomo de México (ITAM)
John F.H. Purcell, Salomon Brothers
Riordan Roett, Johns Hopkins University
Hiromoto Seki, Consulate General of Japan
Richard Sinkin, InterAmerican Holdings Co.
Dorothy Sobol, Federal Reserve Bank of New York
Gary L. Springer, Shearman and Sterling
Manuel Suárez-Mier, Georgetown University
Gustavo Vega Canovas, Yale University
Monica Verea Campos, Centro de Investigaciones sobre América del Norte (CISAN)
Jeffrey Werneck, Asesoría Reestructura Financiamiento Empresarial (ARFE)
Dan Wilson, First National Bank of Chicago

Bibliography

Aspe, Pedro, ed. *Political Economy of Income Distribution in Mexico*. London: Holmes and Meier, 1984.

Baer, M. Delal. *Mexico: Politics and the Peso in Transition*. Global Business White Paper Series. Washington, DC: Center for Strategic and International Studies, 1997.

———. "Misreading Mexico," in *Foreign Policy*, fall 1997, pp. 138–150.

Barkin, David. *Distorted Development: Mexico in the World Economy*. Series in Political Economy and Economic Development in Latin America. Boulder: Westview Press, 1995.

Behrman, Jere R. *Human Resources in Latin America and the Caribbean*. Washington, DC: Interamerican Development Bank, 1996.

Blum Valenzuela, Roberto. *De la política mexicana y sus medios: ¿Deterioro institucional o nuevo pacto político?* Mexico City: Centro de Investigación para el Desarrollo, A.C., Grupo Editorial Miguel Angel Porrúa, 1996.

Bresser Pereira, José María Maravall, and Adam Przeworski. *Economic Reforms in New Democracies: A Social-Democratic Approach*. Cambridge: Cambridge University Press, 1993.

Bulmer-Thomas, Victor, ed. *The New Economic Model in Latin America and Its Impact on Income Distribution and Poverty*. New York: St. Martin's Press, 1996.

Camp, Roderic Ai. *Politics in Mexico*. New York: Oxford University Press, 1996.

Castañeda, Jorge. *The Mexican Shock*. New York: New Press, 1995.

Centeno, Miguel A. *Democracy Within Reason: Technocratic Revolution in Mexico*. University Park: Pennsylvania State University Press, 1997.

CIDAC (Centro de Investigación para el Desarrollo, A.C.). *Reforma del sistema político mexicano: Condición para la modernización*. Mexico City: Editorial Diana and CIDAC, Serie Alternativas para el Futuro, 1990.

Cook, María Lorena, Kevin J. Middlebrook, and Juan Molinar Horcasitas, eds. *The Politics of Economic Restructuring: State-Society Relations and Regime Change in Mexico*. U.S.-Mexico Contemporary Perspectives Series no. 7. La Jolla: Center for U.S.-Mexico Studies, University of California at San Diego, 1994.

Cornelius, Wayne A. *The Political Economy of Mexico Under de la Madrid: The*

Crisis Deepens, 1985–1986. La Jolla: Center for U.S.-Mexico Studies, University of California at San Diego, 1986.

Cornelius, Wayne A., Ann L. Craig, and Jonathan Fox, eds. *Transforming State-Society Relations in Mexico: The National Security Strategy.* U.S.-Mexico Contemporary Perspectives Series no. 6. La Jolla: Center for U.S.-Mexico Studies, University of California at San Diego, 1994.

Díaz Cayeros, Alberto, *Desarrollo Económico e Inequidad Regional: Hacia un Nuevo Pacto Federal.* Mexico City: Centro de Investigación para el Desarrollo, A.C., and Editorial Miguel Angel Porrúa, 1995.

Dominguez, Jorge I. *Mexico's Political Economy.* Beverly Hills: Sage, 1982.

Fuentes, Carlos. *Por un progreso incluyente.* Mexico City: Instituto de Estudios Educativos y Sindicales de América (IEESA), 1997.

Gíl Díaz, Francisco, and Agustin Carstens. "Some Hypotheses Related to the Mexican 1994–95 Crisis," in *American Economic Review,* May 1996.

Graham, Carol. *Safety Nets, Politics and the Poor.* Washington, DC: Brookings Institution, 1994.

Grayson, George. *Mexico: Corporatism to Pluralism.* Fort Worth: Harcourt-Brace Publishers, 1997.

Ibarra, David. *Transición o Crisis?: Las contradicciones de la política económica y el bienestar social.* Mexico City: Editorial Aguilar, 1996.

Krauze, Enrique. *Biography of Power: A History of Modern Mexico, 1810–1996.* New York: HarperCollins, 1997.

Levy, Daniel C., and Emilio Zebadúa. *Mexico: The Struggle for Democratic Development.* Nations of the Modern World: Latin America Series. Boulder: Westview Press, 1997.

Lustig, Nora. *Coping with Austerity: Poverty and Austerity in Latin America.* Washington, DC: Brookings Institution, 1994.

———. *Mexico: The Remaking of an Economy.* Washington, DC: Brookings Institution, 1992.

Maddison, Angus. *The Political Economy of Poverty, Equity and Growth: Brazil and Mexico, a World Bank Comparative Study.* New York: Oxford University Press, 1992.

Martinez, Gabriel, and Guillermo Farber. *Desregulación económica, 1989–1993.* Mexico City: Fondo de la Cultura Económica (FCE), 1994.

Morris, Stephen D. *Political Reformism in Mexico: An Overview of Contemporary Mexican Politics.* Boulder: Lynne Rienner Publishers, 1995.

Ortíz Martinez, Guillermo. *La reforma financiera y la desincorporación bancaria.* Mexico City: Fondo de Cultura Económica (FCE), 1994.

Philip, George, ed. *The Mexican Economy.* London: Routledge, 1988.

Psacharolpoulos, George, Samuel Morley, Ariel Fiszbein, Haeduck Lee, and Bill Wood. *Poverty and Income Distribution in Latin America: The Story of the 1980s.* Washington, DC: World Bank, 1992.

Purcell, Susan Kaufman. "The Interdependence of Political and Economic Reforms in Mexico," *SAIS Review,* winter/spring 1995, pp. 1–13.

———. "Mexico." In *Latin American Politics and Development, Fourth Edition.* Howard J. Wiarda and Harvey F. Kline, eds. Boulder: Westview Press, 1996, pp. 343–369.

Rodríguez, Victoria. *Decentralization in Mexico.* Boulder: Westview Press, 1997.

Roett, Riordan. *Challenge of Institutional Reform in Mexico.* Boulder: Lynne Rienner Publishers, 1995.

————. *The Mexican Peso Crisis: International Perspectives.* Boulder: Lynne Rienner Publishers, 1996.

Rubio, Luis. *Information, Citizenship and Public Policy.* Mexico City: Editorial Miguel Angel Porrua (forthcoming).

————. "The Mexican Democratic Quandary." *Emerging Markets Research Latin America.* New York: Salomon Brothers, August 1994.

Rubio, Luis, Beatriz Magaloni, and Edna Jaime. *A la puerta de la ley: El estado de derecho en México.* Mexico City: Editorial Cal y Arena and Centro de Investigación para el Desarrollo, A.C., 1994.

Teichman, Judith A. *Privatization and Political Change in Mexico.* Pittsburgh: University of Pittsburgh Press, 1996.

Tellez Kuenzler, Luis. *La modernización del sector agropecuario y forestal.* Mexico City: Fondo de Cultura Económica (FCE), 1994.

Trejo, Guillermo, and Claudio Jones. *Contra la pobreza: Por una estrategia de política social.* Mexico City: Editorial Cal y Arena and Centro de Investigación para el Desarrollo, A.C., 1993.

Vélez, Felix, ed. *La pobreza en México: Causas y políticas para combatirla.* Mexico City: Instituto Tecnológico Autónomo de México (ITAM) and Fondo de Cultura Económica (FCE), 1994.

Weintraub, Sidney. *Transforming the Mexican Economy: The Salinas Sexenio.* Washington, DC: Mexican National Planning Commission, 1990.

Wilkie, James W., ed. *Society and Economy in Mexico.* Statistical Abstract of Latin America Supplement Series no. 10. Los Angeles: University of California at Los Angeles, 1990.

The Contributors

Mauricio A. González Gómez is general director of the Grupo de Economistas y Asociados (GEA), an independent political and economic consulting firm in Mexico City. He studied economics at the Instituto Tecnológico Autónomo de México (ITAM) and is a Ph.D. candidate in economics at the University of Chicago. He has been a professor at ITAM and at the Universidad Iberoamericana, and he worked for several years at the Ministry of Finance and in Mexico's banking system. He collaborates monthly on GEA's publications about economic and political developments in Mexico.

Claudio Jones is a research associate at the Centro de Investigación para el Desarrollo, A.C. (CIDAC) in Mexico City. He is coauthor with Guillermo Trejo and CIDAC of *Educación para una economía competitiva*, a volume on elementary education and educational reform in contemporary Mexico. Also with Guillermo Trejo, he coordinated the writing and publication of *Contra la pobreza*, on social policy reform in Mexico. Jones is also currently a doctoral student at Columbia University.

Susan Kaufman Purcell is vice president of the Americas Society and Council of the Americas in New York City. Between 1981 and 1988 she was a senior fellow and director of the Latin American Project at the Council on Foreign Relations. She was also a member of the U.S. State Department's Policy Planning Staff, with responsibility for Latin America and the Caribbean, between 1980 and 1981. Dr. Purcell received her M.A. and Ph.D. from Columbia University and was previously a professor of political science at the University of California, Los Angeles. She is a director of the Argentina Fund, the Scudder Global High Income Fund, and Valero Energy Corporation

141

and sits on the boards of the National Endowment for Democracy and Freedom House. Most recently, she coedited and contributed to *Brazil Under Cardoso* (1997).

Luis Rubio is president of the Centro de Investigación para el Desarrollo, A.C. (CIDAC), an independent research institution in Mexico City. He holds a Ph.D. from Brandeis University and a diploma in financial management. In addition, Rubio is a member of the boards of directors of the Human Rights Commission of Mexico City and of the Mexico Equity and Income Fund.

Guillermo Trejo is a research associate at the Centro de Investigación y Docencia Económicas (CIDE), a research institution in Mexico City, and a doctoral student in the Department of Economics at the University of Chicago. Previously, as a research associate at the Centro de Investigación para el Desarrollo, A.C. (CIDAC), he edited two publications with Claudio Jones, *Educación para una economía competitiva* and *Contra la pobreza*.

Index

143

About the Book

Following a turbulent year of political and social upheaval, Ernesto Zedillo Ponce de León was inaugurated as Mexico's president in December 1994. Soon thereafter, the collapse of the peso forced a reorientation of the country's political, economic, and social policies and priorities, with the new vulnerability of the long-entrenched PRI regime reflected in the 1997 mid-term elections.

Mexico Under Zedillo examines Mexico's accelerated movement toward democracy during this period, considering the political dilemmas facing the country, the structures and functions of its traditional political institutions (and how they began to unravel), the evolution of the presidency, and the crucial question of how political parties will cope with ongoing change. The authors also assess Mexico's economic outlook for the medium and long term; as well as the politics of its social policy, focusing on poverty and income distribution, social policy strategies since 1982, and the political challenges posed by the decentralization of political power. The final chapter discusses the changing U.S.-Mexico relationship.

Susan Kaufman Purcell is vice president of the Americas Society and Council of the Americas. **Luis Rubio** is president of CIDAC (Centro de Investigación para el Desarrollo, A.C.), an independent research institution in Mexico City.